DIFFERENT CLASS

DIFFERENT CLASS

The Story of Schools Rugby League

Phil Caplan
Ron England

Scratching Shed Publishing Ltd

Copyright © Ron England, Phil Caplan 2014
All rights reserved
The moral right of the author has been asserted

First published by Scratching Shed Publishing Ltd in 2014
Registered in England & Wales No. 6588772.
Registered office:
47 Street Lane, Leeds, West Yorkshire. LS8 1AP

www.scratchingshedpublishing.co.uk

ISBN 978-0956804341

No part of this book may be reproduced or transmitted in any form or by any other means without the written permission of the publisher, except by a reviewer who wishes to quote brief passages in connection with a review written for insertion in a magazine, newspaper or broadcast

All photographs are © the contributors

A catalogue record for this book is available from the British Library.

Typeset in Cheltenham Bold and Palatino

Printed and bound in the United Kingdom by
Charlesworth Press, Flanshaw Way, Flanshaw Lane,
Wakefield, WF2 9LP

Contents

Acknowledgements

The production of this book has been made possible by a grant from the Awards for All Lottery Fund and the RFL Heritage Fund. Without this financial support, it could not have been so extensively researched and published. We are extremely grateful.

A massive thank you is necessary to everyone who responded to our calls for information. People of all ages, from all over the country have sent in their memories.

Additionally, to those in every area who ferreted out material on our behalf which has been so valuable in piecing together the full story, and is intended to be the start of a permanent, living archive for each region.

Special mention is necessary to John Maloney, a proud member of the St John Fisher, Dewsbury, school team that won the Yorkshire Schools Cup in 1960/61 and John Arundel interviewer extraordinaire, for keeping the inspiration going.

Pictures have come from a variety of sources and eras which makes acknowledgement extremely difficult. If any copyright has been breached, it is entirely unintentional.

*

Foreword
By Neil Fox, MBE

Schools rugby league is the lifeblood of the game. I certainly couldn't have achieved what I did without the grounding I got playing for our local school in Sharlston. It took pupils right the way through from age four to fifteen and both my elder brothers, Peter and Don, played there before me so there was a family history and tradition to uphold.

I started playing for the school's U11s when I was eight so I got an early introduction. As my dad and brothers all became professional players I already had a good grounding but I got a lot of help and encouragement from my teachers, particularly Mr Musgrave, who was the sport's master and eventually became the head.

Joby Musgrave and his wife Betty took a real interest in the rugby league team and organised our trips to away games down to the last detail. They were practically a second set of parents to me and the other lads.

I always played in the backs at school and was settled at centre by the time I was in the intermediates (U13s) although I was only eleven. Two years later I was playing for the U15s senior side. Sharlston School was classed as being in the Castleford district so we played rivals from places like Featherstone, Cas and Normanton. A lot of the boys I played with or against in those days went on to have good careers in the professional game and it was obvious that this was a

Yorkshire County Schools prepare to face Lancashire County Schools in 1954. Neil Fox is front row, fourth from left

fantastic breeding ground for talent. When I was fourteen, I got the picked for the Castleford Town side and then I was selected as captain of Yorkshire Schools, a huge honour. Sadly, we lost to Lancashire at St Helens but then again they had two half backs called Alex Murphy and Jackie Edwards.

We had some cracking players too; Ken Hirst, who was only thirteen and went on to play on the wing for Wakefield, international hooker Barry Simms who helped win Leeds' first title, and future Hull K.R. duo John Taylor – who I went on tour with in 1962 - and Dave Elliott.

I was picked for the next Yorkshire Schools game when we beat Cumberland at Dewsbury. Those matches were the highlights of my schooldays.

My sporting abilities were definitely greater than my academic talents and I'll always be grateful for my involvement in school sports, especially rugby league.

NEIL FOX, MBE

*

Introduction
by Ron England

Schools began playing organised rugby league against each other at the turn of the last century. This book is the first attempt to capture their remarkable story, one that covers both the traditional areas where the sport has been historically strong – the northern, industrial towns and cities - and, more recently, in development areas that have seen enormous growth.

It is dedicated to all those teachers who have given so freely of their time and had the vision, dedication and commitment to further the rugby league cause. The memories of them and pride in shared achievements remain treasured by their charges and so many are still spoken of with awe long after their reign of influence has passed.

A key feature of English education has always been the playing of team games. The training and selection of teams, organizing fixtures and combining with colleagues to form local, regional and, ultimately, a national structure has been a lifelong passion for innumerable educationalists, many of them unsung, and this is certainly true for rugby league.

It is an oft-repeated comment from many ex-pupils interviewed for the book that it was rugby and playing for the school team that kept them motivated and on the straight-and-narrow while for teachers the chance to discover a talented player, foster character, unlock potential

Rugby league administrator Ron England pictured far right with fellow Olympic Torch bearers in Hull on June 18, 2012

and build a successful team was, and still remains, high on the list of what makes the job enjoyable.

Although this is not a chronology, to understand the reminiscences, there is a need for context.

When the split came in rugby in 1895, ostensibly over broken-time payments, it did so along class lines. Schools attended by working class kids followed their towns and cities into the Northern Union, which was to become rugby league.

Soon after, the founding fathers of schools rugby league began forming teams. They were passionate about their sport. They lived in the same communities as the boys in their teams. They had fierce local pride and responded to the local rivalries of other schools, usually only streets away.

The living conditions in the primarily industrial towns were often harsh and brutal. Low pay, unemployment, poor diet and cramped housing were the norm. Everyone shared in the adversity and struggled to get by.

Playing out on the streets until they were called in was the way boys socialised. Skills were acquired and lifelong friendships formed. It was this safe closeness which helped the school teams to succeed.

Among the first recorded, Leeds schools set up their association in 1902 and established the Goldthorpe Trophy which is still played for. By 1905, 12 schools were playing in the Wigan Schools League.

In 1912, the winner of the first Yorkshire Schools Cup was South Crosland from Huddersfield who defeated Hull's Lincoln Street in the final. In the same year the Yorkshire and Lancashire Schools Associations were formed and the inaugural inter-county match played the following season.

The famous Hunslet Schools Association was established at the start of the twenties. Photos of the formidable Hunslet Carr sides of that era are displayed in the local Morrisons store. Players and teams became known and respected and have now a place in the area's folklore.

The local school association handbooks show that the early teachers took their roles very seriously and the rules, regulations and the moral aspect of the sport were laid out very clearly.

In 1926 the first *Daily Dispatch* Shield final was played at Central Park, Wigan where local boys St Patricks defeated Widnes St Bedes in front of a 16,000 crowd. Eight years later, The St Helens Town Team toured France, playing games In Paris and Bordeaux. The pioneering bedrock of schools rugby league was being enshrined.

A national governing body for schools rugby league was formed in 1967, bringing together the Lancashire and Yorkshire Schools Regional Associations to form the English Schools Rugby League.

No time was wasted in sending the first representative team to play in France and so began a great and long-lasting relationship, which was the first taste of the continental life for many boys and teachers alike with its culture shock of pastis, garlic, unsliced bread and 15-year-olds with beards. Goodness knows what the French thought of the English, particularly the teachers!

By 1972, ESRL was sufficiently well organized to welcome the inaugural, eye-opening Australian Schoolboys to these shores and, in 1999, we flew out to Queensland for the first time with a team that included Rob Burrow, Sean O'Loughlin and Danny McGuire.

By then, the structure of education had changed, with implications for sport, especially at Secondary level.

In the beginning, the All-Age schools were established to give a basic education to working class children. They served neighbourhoods, were free from exams and included all the basic non-academic subjects such as crafts, cooking and sports.

Although most schools had no fields, kids would practice in the school yard or with robust games in the gym. This would supplement the skills which the boys had already developed through hours of play on the streets with their mates.

The movement into the Secondary Modern/Grammar School system served to more clearly define the working class roots of the game. The reward for the academically bright boy was a place at the local Grammar School, with its Academic curriculum and House systems.

They did not play against the Secondary Moderns but had their own fixture structures and preferred sports. Rugby league was definitely not one of them.

At the Secondary's there were no exams to worry about with timetables based more on vocational skills. Schools RL thrived there. They were community-based focal points, embellishing old, local rivalries on the field.

In the late 1950s and early '60s a growing unease about this 'sheep and goats' approach to secondary education eventually lead to the introduction of the Comprehensive School.

In a bold move at social engineering, all pupils were now to go to the same school for their secondary education. The curriculum would include items from both Modern and Grammar schools, but with the emphasis on meeting the expectations of a more aspirational society, by offering all pupils the chance to get exam qualifications and to enjoy the same facilities and expenditure.

This move was largely popular but it had ramifications for schools rugby league. Competitive sport slipped down the agenda although the game still had a presence at school, county and national level.

However, such schools suffered from low esteem and morale, became underfunded and fell victim to disputes with the government about teachers pay and conditions.

Those who had hitherto given countless hours of their own time to train school teams and sustain a massive inter-school sports structure, were now required to begin counting their hours of work and filling in forms to verify their efforts.

That was the last straw for many, whose response was to give up those extras which were not valued by the government.

The sport was heading for a period of turmoil. The need for junior clubs was obvious, they were successful and for the most part relations between teachers and local clubs run under the auspices of the newly-created British Amateur Rugby League Association were good.

They both had the interests of the boys at heart. The problem was that both organisations needed the same players at the weekend. Political wrangling meant that those who suffered were the boys themselves who were now becoming overplayed and over trained.

Eventually, in the late 90s, the Rugby Football League convened a Youth Commission and created the Service Area structure based on the old educational boundaries, run by full time officers. They brought together all the different RL organisations within the area in order to plan strategically to take the game forward.

The Service Areas were to assume control of all representative outfits although, in theory, the ESRL national teams would remain, with the assistance of the RFL Performance Department. It was an uneasy compromise which eventually saw the demise of those representative sides.

This settlement was a huge challenge to the schools game. At a stroke they had lost the jewels in their crown, Inter-Town and Inter-County clashes. It was a moment which has defined progress to the present day.

The ESRL started its Champion Schools Competition in 1981. It was initially competed for by schools from Yorkshire, Lancashire and Cumbria but was revamped to go national in 2002 which, for the first time, brought huge funding into the schools game, first from Powergen and then Leeds Metropolitan University through their world-renowned Carnegie brand, and supported by the RFL.

At a stroke the traditional regions were joined by the North East, London/South, Midlands, Wales and Scotland and subsequently the South West.

Each region would have the same structure from local through regional to national and teams reaching the increasingly high profile finals received new playing kits, high quality medals, photographs and DVD's of their exploits and in-put from the professional club in their area. Coach transport in the national rounds is subsidised so that teams have the great experience of playing all over the country.

Oakwood Primary, Warrington at the end of a wonderful season. Back row (left to right) Dave Hardman, Wayne Gaskell, Rodney Gilmour, Roy Hough, Steve Dickinson, Alan Crooks, Stuart Smith, Kenny Algie. Front Row (left to right) Philip Cullen, Pete Bilsborough, John Morris, Gordon Sloane, Kenny Furnival, Keith Leah, Steve McWhirter.

Champion Schools has been a massive hit for students, parents, schools and the whole game. It has delivered high quality at all levels and has led to hundreds more schools playing league.

It has also shown that people in all parts of the country can play, enjoy and support the game. It is no longer necessary to be born or live in the north of England to excite and excel at it and the competition truly reflects our cosmopolitan nature, encompassing boys and girls of every ethnic background.

Champion Schools has further illustrated to the wider game that its major selling point remains the inherently attractive nature of the sport itself with its speed of mind and body, athleticism, total involvement, enjoyment of physical contact and creativity.

The success of introducing girls has been particularly rewarding. We now have our most talented year 11s going straight into the England Women's squad.

Every type of school now plays rugby league. Champion Schools, in particular, has brought new supporters into the game. The old prejudices on both sides of the rugby divide have been dispelled as many of the new schools play both codes at a high level.

Brynteg High from Bridgend won the Y7 title against Castleford High at the Millennium Stadium in 2005. St Josephs of Swansea beat Temple Moor from Leeds in the Y8 final at Wembley in 2011. In 2010, Brentwood County High School from Essex were narrowly beaten in the year 8 decider by Outwood Grange Academy from Wakefield.

Memorably, two years later, the first southern team to win a national schools title was Howard of Effingham from Leatherhead, Surrey when they beat Castleford High at Wembley; RGS High Wycombe emulating their feat the following year.

Like the boys, the girls come from every background. They have brought excitement and exuberance and a great level of fair play to the game. The honour of being the first Girls Champion School went to Queensbury in Bradford while among the first Girls National finalists at Y8 were Feltham Community College from Hounslow.

In 2013, Leigh Academy – not from Lancashire but Dartford in Kent - won the Girls year 9 crown. These are important modern milestones that build on the previous 100 or so years.

All the accomplishments of the players in Champion Schools would have been impossible without the input of young match officials who have been able to thrive and progress in the ethos of the schools game.

The competition – believed to be the largest of its kind in the sport worldwide - has caught the imagination of all involved and given our sport great credibility.

Many things have changed but shared passion for the game remains one of its strengths. Teachers who have been involved still eagerly follow the careers of former pupils, be they amateurs, professionals or internationals.

The best-known players still have fond memories of their teachers and schools and early teammates who themselves take great pride in having played alongside those who reached the top.

Every league playing area could write its own colourful story of schools RL. This game has developed great characters both on and off the field. This bank of memories, some awe-inspiring, others comic, many seemingly ordinary but of social importance embody the spirit of the game and the never-to-be forgotten camaraderie it offers.

For the teachers, the constant challenge of building the school team, discovering those talents that make the heart beat faster and maintaining the reputation of the school in the community remain, even today when education seems to equate with different league tables.

Just as when schools rugby league was formed and there were issues of malnutrition and inadequate facilities, there is now a growing need to address current health and social problems caused by an increasingly inactive and largely sedentary population. In particular, the very apparent issues of obesity and social exclusion among young people, which are going to prove very expensive for the National Health Service further down the line.

Competitive school sport is back at the top of the agenda. Perhaps the schoolteachers posing in their bowler hats proudly alongside their school teams, were right all along. Competitive sport is character building and life enhancing. In education, the wheel soon comes full circle.

But this book is not about politics.

I have had the pleasure of looking at hundreds of school team photos during this project, with their cups and rows of medals and vibrant, proud, happy faces. Those taken of school teams today continue that theme and provide a visual link with the past.

Over the time period of this book, society, work, lifestyles and expectations have changed dramatically. The game of rugby league has lived through those changes. Somewhere, someone today will be opening the door for a pupil to enjoy a life involving rugby league at its heart.

It may now occur in Kent, Surrey, Birmingham, Cardiff, Newcastle, London or Glasgow as well as all the traditional areas. It may now be for a girl as well as a boy.

I have had the great good fortune to be involved in schools rugby league as a supporter, teacher, coach and administrator for over 60 years. The opportunity was given by my late uncle Fred, who was the St John's Ambulance man at Odsal Stadium, Bradford in the late 1940s.

Sitting with him on a wooden bench at the side of the pitch, I watched the great Northern side including Ernest Ward, Trevor Foster, Jack Kitching and Ken Trail. I was hooked and have never forgotten the smell when the changing room door opened at the top of the Odsal steps.

I taught at Knottingley High for over 20 years in the 1970s and 80s and was involved with Castleford Schools for all that time. We had boys with fantastic skill and hearts like lions.

The school rugby team is very important to the

reputation of the school and the town and its spin offs in terms of developing young leaders, volunteers and match officials makes it a complete educational package which fits perfectly with the current policies on inter-school competitive sport.

School's rugby league has adjusted to good times and bad, to government involvement or disinterest, to indifference or support from the educational establishment or governing body.

Expectations are now much higher in every aspect of life, particularly in education and leisure. What was acceptable 50 years ago is no longer an option.

Certainly the schools game is unrecognisable from its early beginnings, the growing affluence and leisure choices now would have astounded the boys and teachers in those initial school teams.

If the pupils in the early pictures could come back they would be puzzled and amazed at the game today but they would take full advantage of the opportunities currently on offer.

It would be very gratifying for the pioneer teachers to see how far the game has progressed and that their values and ideals - of sport bringing health and lifelong enjoyment, community spirit and personal development - continue to underpin it.

They set in motion one of the great school sports. Each succeeding generation has taken up the challenge to continue to develop the game and move with the times.

All involved over the years; teachers, pupils, parents and supporting bodies, can take pride from their association. Long may it continue.

RON ENGLAND
Knottingley High, Castleford Schools,
Yorkshire Schools, English Schools

Dewsbury St John Fisher, triumphant in 1960-1. Back row (left to right) Mr T. Morrell, N. Speight, D. O'Connor, A. Seeling, M. Berry, M. Oates, A. Curley, K. Hayes, K. McMahon, Mr D.S. Brown. Seated (left to right) B. Watson, M. Hunt, J. Maloney, D. Kaye (capt), J. Dransfield, T. Grabbe, P. Curnin.

*

Preface
by Phil Caplan

This book is intended to be commemorative but is not about results or records; it tells a story and offers a wider social history about the most unsung area of rugby league, the one on which its very foundations are built.

It attempts to provide a context and capture the flavour of the many and varied contributors to the history of schools rugby league rather than be a list of medal winners, more 'When Push Comes to Shove' than 'Rothmans Year Book'.

It is a frequently changing tale of achievement, be that in responding to societal changes, merely finding and taking the field or representing the country.

Selflessness and dedication remain the constants throughout, along with a pioneering, indefatigable spirit.

All of those qualities are embodied by Ron England, without whom this homage would not have come to fruition. As well as scouring any possible recesses for information and reminiscence, his spirit and constant enthusiasm in driving the project was contagious and is hopefully reflected in these pages.

Four years in the making - two to gather Pandora's Boxes full of memories and images and a further two to piece it together - the project was always intended to be a two-fold legacy enterprise; creating a living, on-going archive for all of the regions to build upon, and this volume that offers a snapshot of it.

Over 60 boxes of material were collected nationwide; a mountain of minute books, articles, reports, programmes, pictures and brochures. They were added to with appeals for members of the public to send in their tales together with interviews with some of those who played a significant part in or where products of the schools game, many of whom went on to have successful professional playing careers.

But this is as much about those whose sole glory was on a lone school field as it is any budding superstar, recounting where rugby league made a mark in formative years and instilling as much a life lesson as a sporting one.

In putting the chapter themes together, and inevitably there are crossovers within them, the idea was to mix fact with anecdote, to illustrate the human side of the story, to pay tribute to visionaries whatever the geography or prevailing social conditions of the time.

It has two stands, the visual – and merely by looking at the changing kits and faces tells a tale – and narrative which is deliberately eclectic so that the book can be delved into on any page to trigger a memory or raise a nod or smile of recognition.

Wherever possible names and spellings have been double-checked but there are inevitable anomalies, two 'A. Holmes' are listed in the Dewsbury & Batley squad for Wembley in 1983, for example and at times it would have needed a graphologist to unpick some of the handwritten notes.

There is something rewarding and exciting in such a voyage of discovery, to trace the start of what became more famous names, to see the first rung on their particular ladder, to uncover, say, that the cherubic faced Cyril Morrell in the all-conquering Hunslet Carr side of 1924-5 was scoring in myrtle and flame as Hunslet won at Wembley ten years later for the only time.

Or that Warrington, Leeds, Huddersfield and Bradford star Neil Harmon did indeed begin his rugby life as a stand off, as all props say they do.

By including sections on community, neighbourhood rivalries, overcoming the odds and trips into the unknown, not only is there a sense of the pioneering spirit that has characterised school rugby league, and the role played by teachers as mentors and personalities, but that this is the recording of a true code of honour.

More meticulous records were kept in places like Wigan, Leeds, Castleford, Dewsbury and, in the early days of its development, London but, hopefully, the tales chosen are truly representative and have a universal resonance, as do the pictures in what has been a constantly moving feast.

Putting it together has been a joy, akin to being deposited in and allowed to ferret around a seemingly endless treasure trove. It has been like fashioning the pieces of a jigsaw. While acknowledging that the pictures and artefacts from the early years consisted mainly of team shots, these have been supplemented by documents, programmes.

More accurately – and, in some ways, appropriately – it has been like mining for gems.

It is intended to pay tribute to some re-occurring names who obviously made a huge impact both in furthering the sport and on those who came under their spell, extending advice and inspiration in equal measure and dispensing opportunity.

Inevitably, though, some will have been missed but this is an attempt to capture their spirit, carried on nowadays by the likes of those guiding Surrey's Howard of Effingham or the Royal Grammar School at High Wycombe as much as it still is at Castleford Academy.

Delving into the past to help make sense of the present has been a privilege for someone who is entranced by the history and roots of rugby league.

Hopefully that pleasure has been conveyed.

Politicians have constantly scrutinised the value of competitive school sport, indeed as this project was taking shape in 2010, the coalition government threatened to scrap it.

If they still need convincing of its worth then, perhaps, the definitive answers as to its undoubted, ongoing merit are contained here.

PHIL CAPLAN,
JANUARY 2014

1
*
Humble Origins

By means of carefully-taken statistics, teacher trainers of Rugby School Teams have proved that the handling game develops a boy's physique as no other game can. It is not just the super-boy for whom Schools Rugby caters, but the average British schoolboy, sound in wind and limb, and possessing the will to give and take hard knocks in the course of a game, which is designed for clean vigour. In every team there is a place for a stalwart forward, a diminutive half-back, and a fleet-footed winger, so that all types of boys are provided with an organised game, which is remarkably free from restraint in movement, for arms as well as legs and feet must be brought into full exercise. The newcomer will speedily find that he lacks the stamina to maintain the fast pace of an hour's play, but if he perseveres, he will discover that fatigue seems to lessen as he progresses with the game. Speed he must have, to keep up with a movement, or to get out of a tight corner. Therefore, enter into the spirit of the game with zest, lead a simple life, develop stamina with long walks, and speed with sharp bursts 'Out of the hole.' In the organised games period, master the rudiments of the game first, learn to pass to the right with the left foot forward and vice versa; forsake the practice of kicking with the instep, which is a 'Soccer' shot, and use the toe instead. When passing, swing the body from

Harry Fletcher's medals - a pupil of Bramley National

the hips with a rhythmic movement free from jerk, and aim the ball midway between your chum's neck and knee. In tackling go 'Low, low, every time' and you will soon delight in bringing down your biggest opponent unerringly.

Notes on Rugby Football for Boys, Syd Walmsley - July 1934

There is an *Examiner* article on January 8th, 1918 where Harold Wagstaff a Captain of England refereed a match between Huddersfield and Wakefield and was asked by one of the boys contesting his decision 'what he knew about the game'! St Patricks one of the smallest won the Yorkshire Schools cup in 1919-20. They also played a 'missionary game' against a combined Halifax team. In 1920 the first inter-town games took place against Leeds, Rochdale and Oldham. Teams' travel was by 'motor charabanc'. By 1923 Yorkshire County were granting £15 for the season but Huddersfield were getting great support from the professional club from collections and donations, a special team of collectors were appointed and brought in almost £35. In 1926 Hillhouse Central won the Yorkshire Cup and Fartown organised a celebration game of Hillhouse v The Rest. A presentation evening was held at Fartown Trinity Wesleyan Sunday School and the Mayor Sir Joseph Turner attended, Dougie Clark presented the trophies. Most of the Rests team were Hillhouse boys. In 1934 Mr Lockwood and Mr Hoyle of the Fartown committee expressed their concerns about the lack of teacher-interest in Schools Rugby and circulars were sent to all schools advertising the game. In 1935 Mr Ashburner of St Helens wrote to ask if Huddersfield were interested in a curtain-raiser at Wembley - it was agreed as long as the R.L. allowed it - nothing came of this. In 1937 it was suggested that a trip for the Wembley Final should be organised and schools invited. It cost 15 shillings or 1 shilling and 3 pence a week. An injured boy from Meltham was given half the cost of the Dr's bill i.e. (12/6) because of poor home circumstances. 1947; £30 was given by Yorkshire County to restart the League. Fartown gave £30 and promised schools needing jerseys to provide 'clothing' coupons to help. Town boys players during 1947 were given pen-knives as mementoes. In 1950 Yorkshire Schools refused to grant any money to Huddersfield because of the monies they received from Fartown R.L. Concern was expressed at the number of town boys fixtures affecting school team fixtures and this was compounded by the Intermediate League playing schoolboys against much older boys and a minimum age limit was set.

Huddersfield Schools Minutes - The Early Years

The movement was launched, its only assets being the cordial goodwill of the senior clubs concerned, supplemented by a small donation from each of the clubs and the hearty enthusiasm of teachers in the south-west corner of Lancashire. Tom Phillips of St Helens as the first chairman was both felicitous and auspicious and was one of the pioneers. He was ably seconded by Mr A Charles, of Widnes, and Mr G H Millard, of Wigan. The first Final, held at Warrington between St Helens and Warrington witnessed a huge 'gate' and a stirring game which placed the organisation on a fairly sound financial basis and assured the movement a promising future. The difficulties of the early days were so many and so great that many teachers might have given up the task in despair. Lack of suitable playing fields and inadequate equipment and accommodation were both formidable obstacles. The inclusion of a rule that boys should 'play in boots' is a reminder of the 'safety first' conditions of the early days when boys, rather than miss a game, would play in clogs or in bare or stockinged feet. Among other perplexities there

Courtney Street from Hull reached the YSRL final 11 times between 1913 & 1947. Teacher Stan Adams, centre back, with one of their outstanding sides from the 1920s.

was the problem of a fair adjustment of the 'age limit' rule, for almost every locality had its own 'school leaving age'. Lancashire Schools Rugby League was established in 1913 when Mr Price of Warrington along with teacher representatives from Widnes, Wigan and St Helens agreed to play their town teams against each other. In 1914 the first knock-out competition resulted in the Lancashire Cup winners being Warrington with St Helens as runners-up. The league handbook has always printed its aim in big letters - 'To foster the physical, mental, social and moral development of the schoolboys of Lancashire through the medium of Rugby League Football'.

Lancashire Schools - The First Twenty-Five Years

South Accommodation Road
School Rugby Team
1938-39
Winners of:
Lowthwaite Cup, Cripps Cup
M.V. Cup, Greenwood Cup

We have received great support from both well-known personalities and from grass-roots aficionados of the game, the 'Down South' newsletter, on subscription at £1 per annum, being instrumental in making our existence known in R.L. circles throughout the world. Visiting teams from Newlands Y.C. (Hull), St Helens YMCA, Huyton Tigers, Holy Trinity H.S. (Thornton, N. Liverpool) and York Schools have all provided experienced opposition for our boys who have responded with a marked improvement in their own game. Daneford School's tour to Scotland brought much praise and the Brunswick Boys Club (Fulham) U13s are all set for a pre-season visit to Yorkshire to play a York School and a Hunslet Boys Club side. The pioneering spirit was certainly in evidence when Stockwell Manor School took part in a R.L. competition along with schools from Staffordshire and the North at Butlins Holiday Camp, Minehead, Somerset.

Dave Part, 1979

'Why are we passing with a housebrick sir?' 'Well it will give you a massive advantage when you get going with the real thing' I was told by my first 'coach' Gerard Kane at St Joesph's in 1957. There was a glue factory next to the 'field' and we always gave our opponents a pre-match tour of the rendering tanks; horses' intestines and all. We never passed a lamp-post without selling a dummy, always sidestepped the oncoming traffic.

Rugby league - Wallgate style - Gerry Fitzhenry

In 1900, there were 50 Mines within five miles of the town centre of Wigan, employing more than 30,000 men, so it is little wonder that the 'broken-time payments' issue which had resonated so deeply should manifest itself in the

Lancashire side 1938-9 that trounced Yorkshire 44-3. Standing: Ogden (Oldham), Woolley (Leigh), Metcalf & Clare (St Helens), Williamson & Barrow (Salford) Seated: Wilde (Liverpool) reserve, Gleave (Wigan), Ratcliffe (Leigh), O'Donnell (Wigan), Hart (Widnes), Quennel (Warrington), Roberts (Swinton) reserve. Front: Ritchie (Wigan), Baxter (Leigh).

adoption of the game in the schools of Wigan. In 1906 the local press was reporting that there were twelve schools engaged in competition. The fact that Representative games were taking place as early as 1906 would seem to support the supposition that organised games had been taking place well before.

Ray Unsworth, Schools stalwart

But rugby at this level is not about winning Championships more about planting the seed of enjoyment in the hearts of the youngsters playing it. Teachers who picked them up dusted them down and put them back on the horse when the going was tough. Those who instilled important qualities of honesty, integrity and commitment that helped them further their careers and those who helped to foster self belief and self confidence.

Phil Larder, former Great Britain coach

1955 - It was stated that it cost the school £40 to stage a game home or away. McGarry, a stand off from St Bees, showed plenty of promise but needs to get the ball away more often. Cumberland lost 6-3 against Yorkshire at a waterlogged Recreation Ground. The gate takings were £3-5-0d. Both teams were introduced to the borough's Mayor W J Denvir. It was the first time that the Cumberland players were awarded badges.

1956 - Tournament held on the Rec U13 and U15 organised by Whitehaven Schools Athletic Association. Frank Lahiff who was a RU referee read up on the RL rules and refereed the full competition. It was reported that it was played in good attitude and spirit. It was a pity that the RL and RU clubs could not be the same. Two Whitehaven school teachers who organised the event were 'bitterly disappointed at the attendance.' One shilling was charged for adults and threepence for children. Mr L Heyworth from Carlisle, the President of Cumberland Schools RL attended a meeting with R Fenwick, Cumberland Commissioner. Mr W Penn, Chairman, stated that with the closure of small rural schools to bigger secondary schools the identity had been lost. A gentlemen's agreement was made that RL, RU and soccer games would not clash.

1958 - It was reported that Hunslet had a good coaching set up and there was a fatherly interest in local boys, in the hope that one day some would turn out for Hunslet RLFC. The Hunslet Vice-Chairman and a Club Director accompanied the boys, and also provided the motor coach. A grant of £1000 was available from the RFL for schools in Cumberland, Lancashire and Yorkshire. This money came from the 1954 tour of Australia.

Cumberland Schools minute books

The Goldthorpe Cup is believed to be the oldest Schools Rugby League Competition in the World. It was named in honour of the Goldthorpes to mark both achievements on the field and also the high regard with which the family was held within the local community. On January 15th 1904, Mr T V Harrison, on behalf of the Hunslet Cricket, Football and Athletic Club presented to the schools union the handsome 'Goldthorpe Trophy'. In making the presentation Mr Harrison conveyed to the union the best wishes of the Hunslet Committee in their endeavours to promote schools football.

Leeds & Hunslet Schools brochure

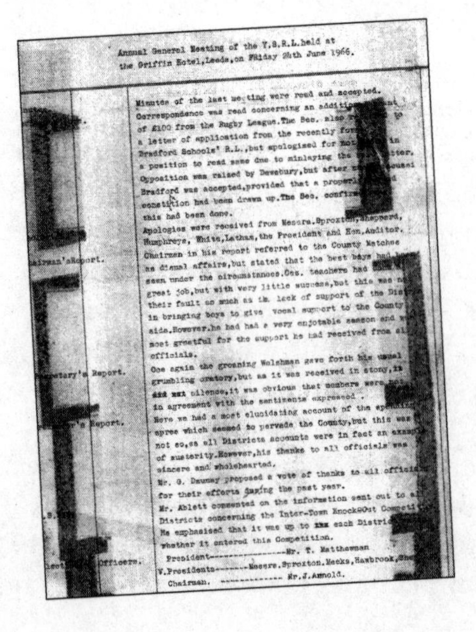

Annual General Meeting of the Y.S.R.L.held at
the Griffin Hotel,Leeds,on FRiday 24th June 1966.

Minutes of the last meeting were read and accepted.
Correspondence was read concerning an additi[illegible]
of £100 from the Rugby League.The Sec. also r[illegible]
a letter of application from the recently for[illegible]
Bradford Schools' R.L.,but apologised for not [illegible] in
a position to read same due to mislaying the [illegible]tter.
Opposition was raised by Dewsbury,but after [illegible]
Bradford was accepted,provided that a proper[illegible]
constitution had been drawn up.The Sec. confir[illegible]
this had been done.
Apologies were received from Messrs.Sproxton,Sheppard,
Humphreys, White,Latham,the President and Hon.Auditor.
Chairman's Report. Chairman in his report referred to the County Matches
as dismal affairs,but stated that the best boys had [illegible]
seen under the circumstances.Gen. teachers had [illegible]
great job,but with very little success,but this was n[illegible]
their fault so much as the lack of support of the Dis[illegible]
in bringing boys to give vocal support to the County
side.However,he had had a very enjoyable season and w[illegible]
most greatful for the support he had received from al[illegible]
officials.
Secretary's Report. One again the groaning Welshman gave forth his usual
grumbling oratory,but as it was received in stony,in
silence,it was obvious that members were [illegible]
in agreement with the sentiments expressed .
...'s Report. Here we had a most elucidating account of the sp[illegible]
spree which seemed to pervade the County,but this was [illegible]
not so,as all Districts accounts were in fact an examp[illegible]
of austerity.However,his thanks to all officials was
sincere and wholehearted.
Mr. G. Dawney proposed a vote of thanks to all offici[illegible]
for their efforts during the past year.
Mr. Ablett commented on the information sent out to al[illegible]
Districts concerning the Inter-Town Knock-Out Competi[illegible]
He emphasised that it was up to each Distric[illegible]
whether it entered this Competition.
Officers. President------------------Mr. T. Matthewman
V.Presidents--------Messrs.Sproxton.Meeks,Hawbrook,She[illegible]
Chairman. ------------- Mr.J.Arnold.

Insightful YSL AGM minutes from 1966

An early incarnation of the Champion Schools concept from 1980

I was introduced to schoolboy rugby league in September, 1961, when my young Geography teacher, Mr. Profitt invited all first years to a rugby practice. Practices took place after school because the game was coached not by PE staff in games lessons, but by other schoolmasters giving up their free time. I wasn't appreciative of that point then, and it wasn't until thirteen years later, when I became a schoolmaster myself, that I realised the hard voluntary work involved in encouraging boys to play rugby league. I spent four years under the guidance of Tony Profitt. Rugby league was very strong in the Wakefield area in those days and there was no shortage of boys wanting to emulate their heroes. I was never really any good - I didn't weigh more than two-pennorth of copper - and never really forced my way into a star team which included hooker Tony Handforth and a giant of a boy Hugh Poyner, who also became English Schools' Shot-Put Champion. Nevertheless, thanks to the encouragement of Tony and another member of staff, Peter Leeds, I never lost heart. What I lacked in size and skill, I made up for in technical knowledge. It was through talking to Tony that I came to know the game inside out, and, not long after leaving school I was running my own amateur team 'Thorpe Juniors' before turning to refereeing. There are others involved who do as much for the game as those who do the actual coaching in the schools. There was the mysterious man who took your money at the schoolboy gate at Belle Vue, (the Schools' League provided a gate man and are rewarded with a donation of the amount taken towards their funds). A few years ago, when refereeing a City game at Snapethorpe School, I realised that the man who served the tea and biscuits afterwards was the Headmaster, Mr. John Beardsall. There was a tall father figure to the Association, Mr. P. Morris, whom I remember from my days at school, who did invaluable work before leaving the area.

Ron Needham, Secretary of Wakefield Schools RL

You weren't looked after then, with bumps. It was part and parcel, how they tackled, heavy tackling - there was no swapping the ball over. They had to get it off you. That was the game - keep possession.

Doug Walton, ex-Castleford

A party of 24 boys plus the headmaster and Mr Stan Adams, the teacher in charge of the school rugby team, and Mr Coverdale his assistant visited Wakefield. In the morning they went round the cathedral and other places of interest. In the afternoon, they travelled on to Post Office Road, Featherstone where they played South Featherstone secondary school in the YSRL cup 2nd round. Courtney St won 30 pts to 3.
Sat March 19th 1927

A party of 30 boys visited York by charabanc. In the morning

they visited York Minster and walked on the walls. In the afternoon at Clarence Street ground they played Hill House from Huddersfield in the final of the YSRL cup. In a very tight game Courtney St won 6pts to nil. The victorious party arrived home at 9.30 pm to be met by their jubilant parents and supporters.
Sat May 21st 1927

A party of 66 boys and several other members of staff, visited York in the morning and then travelled on to Headingley Stadium, Leeds where they played Bramley National school in the YSRL final. Courtney St ran out winners 24 pts to nil. They arrived home to a great welcome from local dignitaries and supporters at 10pm.
Sat May 9th 1931

Each year in July there would be a special presentation assembly, when lessons would be suspended for the morning and all the cups, trophies and medals won by the pupils would be presented, often by the Lord Mayor of Hull. A merit day's holiday would then be awarded to the whole school.

Courtney St Boys, Hull - School Log Book

The experience of playing Rugby League football in the schools in the Castleford, Normanton and Featherstone districts during the past winter has been most successful. Hitherto the Association game had been played in most of the schools, and doubts were expressed at a meeting of teachers early in the season as to whether the change over would be desirable. A suggestion was that Soccer should be played for one half of the season and Rugby during the other half, but eventually it was decided to form a Rugby League without delay, 16 clubs joined and interest was fully

IF QUALITY is your GOAL YOU WILL SCORE IF YOU TRY MOORHOUSE'S *Delicious* LEMON CURD AND FRESH FRUIT JAMS

WM. MOORHOUSE & SONS Ltd.,
Sunglow Model Factory - Leeds.

HUNSLET SCHOOLS' RUGBY UNION.

Official Handbook

Season 1934-35.

PRICE - ONE PENNY.

● Hunslet Schools handbook listing trophies and teams.
Facing page: Assorted medals through the eras.

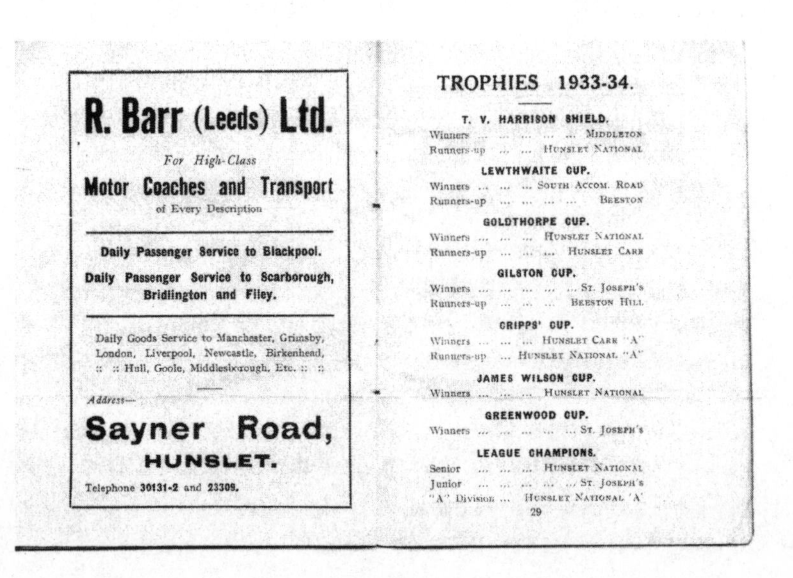

R. Barr (Leeds) Ltd.

For High-Class
Motor Coaches and Transport
of Every Description

Daily Passenger Service to Blackpool.

Daily Passenger Service to Scarborough, Bridlington and Filey.

Daily Goods Service to Manchester, Grimsby, London, Liverpool, Newcastle, Birkenhead, :: :: Hull, Goole, Middlesbrough, Etc. :: ::

Address—
Sayner Road,
HUNSLET.

Telephone 30131-2 and 23309.

TROPHIES 1933-34.

T. V. HARRISON SHIELD.
Winners ... ... Middleton
Runners-up ... ... Hunslet National

LEWTHWAITE CUP.
Winners ... ... South Accom. Road
Runners-up ... ... Beeston

GOLDTHORPE CUP.
Winners ... ... Hunslet National
Runners-up ... ... Hunslet Carr

GILSTON CUP.
Winners ... ... St. Joseph's
Runners-up ... ... Beeston Hill

CRIPPS' CUP.
Winners ... ... Hunslet Carr "A"
Runners-up ... Hunslet National "A"

JAMES WILSON CUP.
Winners ... ... Hunslet National

GREENWOOD CUP.
Winners ... ... St. Joseph's

LEAGUE CHAMPIONS.
Senior ... ... Hunslet National
Junior ... ... St. Joseph's
"A" Division ... Hunslet National 'A'

29

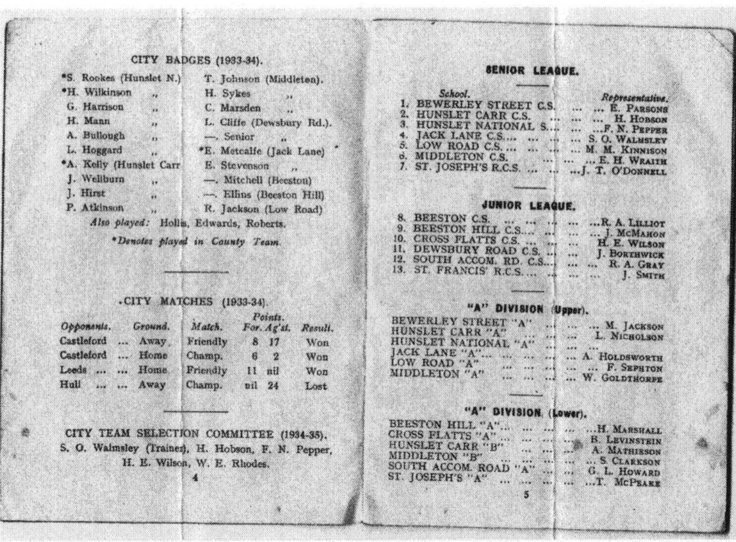

CITY BADGES (1933-34).

*S. Rookes (Hunslet N.)	T. Johnson (Middleton).
*H. Wilkinson ,,	H. Sykes ,,
G. Harrison ,,	C. Marsden ,,
H. Mann ,,	L. Cliffe (Dewsbury Rd.).
A. Bullough ,,	—. Senior ,,
L. Hoggard ,,	*E. Metcalfe (Jack Lane)
*A. Kelly (Hunslet Carr	E. Stevenson ,,
J. Wellburn ,,	—. Mitchell (Beeston)
J. Hirst ,,	—. Ellins (Beeston Hill)
P. Atkinson ,,	R. Jackson (Low Road)

Also played: Hollis, Edwards, Roberts.

**Denotes played in County Team.*

CITY MATCHES (1933-34).

Opponents.	Ground.	Match.	Points. For.	Points. Ag'st.	Result.
Castleford ...	Away	Friendly	8	17	Won
Castleford ...	Home	Champ.	6	2	Won
Leeds	Home	Friendly	11	nil	Won
Hull	Away	Champ.	nil	24	Lost

CITY TEAM SELECTION COMMITTEE (1934-35).

S. O. Walmsley (Trainer), H. Hobson, F. N. Pepper, H. E. Wilson, W. E. Rhodes.

4

SENIOR LEAGUE.

School.	Representative.
1. BEWERLEY STREET C.S.	E. PARSONS
2. HUNSLET CARR C.S.	H. HOBSON
3. HUNSLET NATIONAL S.	F. N. PEPPER
4. JACK LANE C.S.	S. O. WALMSLEY
5. LOW ROAD C.S.	M. M. KINNISON
6. MIDDLETON C.S.	E. H. WRAITH
7. ST. JOSEPH'S R.C.S.	J. T. O'DONNELL

JUNIOR LEAGUE.

School.	Representative.
8. BEESTON C.S.	R. A. LILLIOT
9. BEESTON HILL C.S.	J. McMAHON
10. CROSS FLATTS C.S.	H. E. WILSON
11. DEWSBURY ROAD C.S.	J. BORTHWICK
12. SOUTH ACCOM. RD. C.S.	R. A. GRAY
13. ST. FRANCIS' R.C.S.	J. SMITH

"A" DIVISION (Upper).

School.	Representative.
BEWERLEY STREET "A"	M. JACKSON
HUNSLET CARR "A"	L. NICHOLSON
HUNSLET NATIONAL "A"	
JACK LANE "A"	A. HOLDSWORTH
LOW ROAD "A"	F. SEPHTON
MIDDLETON "A"	W. GOLDTHORPE

"A" DIVISION (Lower).

School.	Representative.
BEESTON HILL "A"	H. MARSHALL
CROSS FLATTS "A"	B. LEVINSTEIN
HUNSLET CARR "B"	A. MATHIESON
MIDDLETON "B"	S. CLARKSON
SOUTH ACCOM. ROAD "A"	G. L. HOWARD
ST. JOSEPH'S "A"	T. McPEAKE

5

Ellenborough School 1948-9 – Back row (left to right) Joe Goodfellow, R. Irving, Jack Ellis, John McKendrie, Norman Garnett, Don Saddler, Alex Wedgwood, Joe Bland, Harry Nixon. Middle row (left to right) Raymond Hewitt, Billy Goodwin, John Baxter, Andy Key, Ike Southward, Jimmy Bland. Seated Luke McTeer (left), Albert Charters.

---

maintained throughout the season. It culminated on Saturday, when South Featherstone succeeded in carrying off the Yorkshire Schools' Championship Cup and medals. Much of the credit for what has been achieved must be given to Mr W B Davies of the Airedale School who, before he came north, played in junior matches in South Wales. One suggestion of his was that a certain number of free tickets for Castleford's home matches should be given to each school, and he urged the officials of the club to reduce the price of admission for schoolboys from 6d. to 2d.

The formation of the Castleford/Featherstone/Normanton Schools RL Association 1932/33

Schoolboy rugby league in Leeds is almost as old as the city of Leeds itself, the first A.G.M. being held after the inaugural season in 1902/3. By the early 1980's the creation of middle schools and the organising of competitions from U9 through to U16 levels helped to swell the total of teams playing to over 100. For over 30 years Leeds and Hunslet Schools ran an annual trip to the Cup Final. Around 500 youngsters and 50 staff travelled by train, had a bus trip around London and saw the match - the first such trip in 1933 cost just 12 shillings. An enlightened decision was made in 1948, when the Leeds and Hunslet Schools' R.L. formed a sub-committee to produce perhaps the first ever rugby league coaching book. It was very well received at the time (with several re-prints) and it is no exaggeration to say that many of the ideas in it influenced the Australian Rugby League when they set up their coaching scheme. As a schoolboy player and Leeds supporter in the mid-60s, I was regaled with the stories of Robin Dewhurst who was a 'superstar' the only time my school, St Michael C/E, won the Cup. As a coach in the early 80s, I can remember my own Holt Park sides facing the outstanding talent of a certain James Lowes at Clapgate.

Stephen Boothroyd, Secretary, Leeds Schools' RL - 1993

The 'squad' won the Schools Rugby League Jackson Shield. 'A chap came to give us extra coaching - Eric Harris, wing threequarter with Leeds - locally known as 'the Toowoomba ghost', because of his speed', said Mr Dakin.

Sandal County Junior School 1937

In September 1978, the Inner London Education Authority (ILEA) Schools ARLA was founded and it was agreed that the Southern Schools and Youth Clubs ARLA should act as a parallel organisation, covering all areas of the South which were not incorporated within the sphere of operation of the ILEA. Being an organisation run entirely by schoolteachers, the ILEA was granted affiliation to the ESRL.

Down South Newsletter

The first recorded rugby league game by a local elementary school team was played at Cross Bank. St Mary's Roman Catholic boys, Batley, lost to Huddersfield St Patrick's boys by eleven points to eight. In the early stages the home team's inexperience of match play was very evident. The full-back kicked like a 'soccer' player; tackling generally was too high and lacked vigour; and the forwards, while doing excellent work in the scrums, failed to back up in the loose.

Schoolboy Rugby League is here –
a memorable match at Batley recorded in the local press

In an age of falling standards of discipline and behaviour, it is important that schoolboys develop a correct sporting attitude. Rugby League Football is an ideal game for this purpose as it encourages good habits on and off the field.

It develops a boy's character in that he has to give and take hard physical knocks in a good spirit; he has to accept a referee's decision without answering back; he learns how to fulfil his task in a team, and how to work hard for the good of his team-mates. He must realise that, although everyone plays the game to win, one must accept defeat in a sporting manner and not look for excuses. Finally, there is a correct attitude to winning, requiring the victorious team to show respect for the feelings of the defeated.

Our game is played in schools not just for the benefit of the elite who are selected for City, County or Country honours, although we are extremely proud of boys who reach the highest levels, but also to give enjoyment and satisfaction to the ordinary school team player and to help him improve his skills and knowledge of the game.

John Ahm - Leeds & Hunslet & Morley SRL Handbook - Chairman's Message

I recall a game against Scarborough at Marble Hill, that the London team was winning convincingly, when Bradley Henry, a prop built like a tank made a break, the Scarborough fullback started chasing him and was catching him until - Bradley turned to him and growled like a Lion - the Scarborough player stopped dead and let Bradley continue on his way to score. At one tournament, I recognised a parent on the sideline wearing a long leather trenchcoat. We realised it was the celebrity gangster Dave Courtney, his boy's team Eaglesfield School won the tournament and it was interesting to see the teacher trying to cope when he was speaking to the lads afterwards and Dave strolled over and pulled out a bunch of 50s and gave the lads about £500 to treat themselves for their efforts.

Phil Jones, mainstay of rugby league development in London

The earliest mention is in 1902, of Inter Town matches with Leeds Schools. Originally Wakefield Schools Rugby League Association was confined to schools within the city limits and those close like Crofton, Stanley and Outwood. These 'borders' continued until the 1973 local government reorganisation when Wakefield Metropolitan District Council was formed. That meant that the two schools associations - Wakefield and Castleford came under the one education authority. However, rivalries continued as the two continued to live a separate existence with Wakefield Schools serving the west of the district and Castleford the east. Around 2002 with interest declining, the Wakefield Metropolitan Schools Rugby League Association was born

'*Daily Dispatch*' Shield winners 1949, Widnes Central Secondary Modern. Back row (left to right) F. Topping, K.Munslow, T. Marshall, J. Hughes, A. Stevens, D. Bee, T. Leigh, H. Daniels, Mr L. Clayton. Front row (left to right) W. Brownlow, J. Davenport, B. Doyle, E. Lewis, B. Jones, J. Gerrard, K. Thompson.

to play formal league matches with finals on all three professional grounds.

Bernie Smith

Formerly, we had two major competitions running under the auspices of the ESRL, the Yorkshire Champion Schools and the North West Counties Champion Schools, which then fed into a national structure. What we have now done is expand that and instead bring in Scotland, Wales, London and the South. What we are trying to do is bring all areas of school rugby league together from modified games at Year 7 to Year 11, but in an exciting higher-profile way. We wanted something that had a regional focus that ultimately fed into a national structure. The Champion Schools was and is that model. We supply schools with coaching and there have been plenty of entrants from non-traditional areas. We have had plenty of success there with schools keen to benchmark themselves against more established opposition. With our help, schools are realising that rugby league is the perfect tool for teaching kids the value of teamwork, loyalty and the work ethic generally. Everything you look for in a team sport is there in rugby league.

Andy Harland – RFL officer, expansion of the current Champion Schools competition

Rugby League headquarters was up at Chapeltown Road, Leeds. Bill Fallowfield was running a course for budding referees. We used to travel once a week by public transport and spend a couple of hours learning the rules and enjoy a pork pie and a bottle of beer in a glass. I then got more used to refereeing through practising in games and lessons and started to take on more of the school matches. We'd done a

Widnes Schoolboys, Lancashire Cup Winners in 1953. Back row: W. Ryder, F. Myler, K. Draper, B. Thornett, T. Arrowsmith, W. Hyland, H. Pinnington, P. Cunningham. Front row: M. Foskin, M. Connolly, J. Bright, D. Smith, J. Pichlilingi.

bit of circuit training at college so I tried to bring a bit of that in and games for handling skills in the gym. The lads who were in the rugby team were very rarely a discipline problem in school. That was noticeable.

Peter Hirst

The ESRL Constitution referred specifically to boys, and therefore the inclusion of a young girl was by strict definition, not permitted. Following a determined campaign by the family, and with the support of many bodies including Members of Parliament, Sports Council and organs of the media covering the printed word, radio and television, the Special General Meeting of 8th January decided that it would over rule its own Constitution and give the green light for Sophie to play at Wembley provided that her parents gave written consent and that the family doctor affirmed that there was no reason why Sophie would be disadvantaged in playing in a mixed game of rugby league.

The question of girls playing in a collision sport had been discussed two years earlier when it was acknowledged that in some schools' games girls were playing for primary teams. ESRL sought medical evidence to assure itself that girls would not be disadvantaged due to factors such as the onset of puberty. The evidence concluded girls were able to compete on equal terms. Once puberty was reached girls would be disadvantaged because of boys' greater density of bone structure and because of possible damage to sensitive areas. There are instances of girls in primary schools attaining puberty, and thus it was reasonable to ask whether a blanket licence could be given for a mixed game in primary schools.

I wrote to Doctor Ros Carbon at the Department of Sports' Medicine, London Hospital Medical College, who is a specialist in women in sport and who has carried out extensive surveys in this area. She kindly sent graphs and statistics showing that in terms of height and weight, girls of primary school age compete more than favourably.

There was no sinister plot by ESRL to debar girls, it was simply that when the Constitution was drawn up it was never thought that girls would wish to take part in mixed games in a collision sport. The Constitution quite simply reflected the attitudes of the times in which it was drawn up. It was accordingly somewhat hurtful, and a little annoying, to hear accusation of bias by ESRL against girls being made by uninformed people. Were those people to listen to the teachers involved in out of school activities, they would have heard genuine concerns being expressed, many of them by female colleagues who wish to retain their own individuality in their own sports without the possible influx of boys who tend to be more aggressive. There is also the unease felt by male colleagues at being in charge of mixed teams.

One cannot be cavalier about such issues and some colleagues felt that they were not at ease with changes to the traditional. After a careful weighing, the Executive decided that to reflect the modern age, the Constitution would be changed to formally allow the playing of mixed games in primary schools and to provide extra competitions for girls' teams should there be a need.

Introduction of Girls Rugby League - a report

Playing at Wembley was unbelievable but to be fortunate to score was just awesome. I remember getting the ball on the half way line and dummying to Kevin Sinfield. I went on to score in the corner and I came away feeling on top of the world. We played a game at the London Wasps ground and I injured my jaw. I was taken to hospital for X rays but everything was fine. I remember Garry Schofield coming to see how I was, which was really good considering he was the current Great Britain captain.

Danny Maun, current professional

Caretakers didn't want you hanging around after. We got off the pitch at half past five and if you happened to get a winter, midweek fixture you had to negotiate at great length. A lot of the teachers didn't like it and often would say, 'You can't have so and so because he's been naughty'. It used to crease myself and Mr O'Neill who'd put in hours and hours. The stumbling blocks weren't getting the kids away from the school. Parents used to be shaking me by the hand at the end of the match. They knew I was giving of my time. Even if I made some appalling refereeing decisions against my own team, they were very helpful indeed. A lot of the lads weren't academic and the lessons weren't geared towards some. I'm sure some would have really gone off the rails unless they'd had a physical outlet.

Roy Homer, school teacher

On Thursday, February 15th, a meeting took place between representatives of the Southern Amateur Rugby League, SSYCARLA and several Northern M.P.s at the House of Commons. Those present included Gordon Anderton, Andrew Wardrop and Dave Part from the Southern Schools association. We were honoured with the presence of Denis Howell, the Sports Minister, who provided us with considerable advice and encouragement. A Parliamentary R.L. association is being formed as a result of this meeting. It appears, thanks to information from the minister, that we may be eligible for Sports Council grant aid. An approach is being made to the King George's Jubilee Trust.

House of Commons

2
*
Communities

Rose Bridge delighted a large and enthusiastic crowd at Central Park, recording a well-deserved victory in the final of the *Daily Dispatch* Schoolboy's Rugby Shield and thus earning what in effect is the title of 'Individual School Champions of Lancashire'. The match introduced us to one of the best schoolboy players seen in Lancashire for years in Lawrenson. Mr J McGuire (Chairman Lancashire Schoolboys' Committee) presiding at the presentation of the trophies, remarked that of the ten seasons in which the *Daily Dispatch* Shield had been played for the Wigan area champions had been successful six times, thereby proving that Wigan was still supreme in schoolboy rugby. In addition to the Shield the *Daily Dispatch* had gold medals and a fountain pen to the winners and silver medals and propelling pencils to the losers. Mr Lionel Berry said the *Daily Dispatch* was particularly interested in the young people of Lancashire and was happy to encourage schoolboy football. Thus ended another successful tournament for the *Daily Dispatch* Shield, which was taken in triumph to Ince, where a large crowd waited to welcome its little 'conquering heroes.'

'Daily Dispatch' Shield Final 1935 - Report

1972-73 showed a decline in take-up for Town Boys. The comprehensive schools may well have caused problems because staff in many schools had to spend more time in the transfers to the new system, this was particularly true with St Augustines who were combining with St Gregory's Grammar to become All Saints. In 1973 a match against an Australian Schools Touring side was arranged for January 17th. Mr O'Hara and Mr Murray were to travel to their camp at Hornsea and bring them to St Augustines for a meal and then the match against a combined Huddersfield, Dewsbury and Bradford team. The weather was appalling and the game was cancelled on the day but the Australians did receive a Mayoral Reception after lunch.

Huddersfield Schools Minutes

One of the great things about teaching at Smawthorne is that it was a mining area and the kids generally didn't get an awful lot of support from parents because they didn't know how to. When I went in to offer them rugby league, I just couldn't believe how they threw themselves into it. If ever we had an away game and I needed transport, absolutely no problem. I was turning people away! I always got the impression that they were so pleased that I was doing something for their kids that they were going to support it whichever way they could.

Keith Breckon

Howard of Effingham Head of PE Shane Birkett and his players dedicated victory in their Wembley curtain-raiser to Marcus Hughes-Hallett. The school, based in Leatherhead, Surrey, went into the Year 7 Steven Mullaney Memorial Trophy game with Castleford Academy reeling from the news that their former pupil had died only two days earlier at the age of 20. The players, who only experienced rugby league for the first time last November, wore overshirts for their warm-up dedicated to his memory - and, after a

Post match, trophy-laden Kirkstall Road School dressing room, 1950s.

minute's silence in his honour, went on to pull off a huge upset with an inspired and emotional 24-22 victory over the experienced Yorkshire side. Birkett said 'The Rugby Football League were fantastic to allow this to happen, and their caring approach has meant a great deal to everyone associated with our school. Marcus will be sadly missed, but I am glad he had his moment of fame at the national stadium at the start of the biggest match in the school's history.'

'Schoolboys Dedicate Victory', League Express August 2012

In 1922 St Patrick's and Scot Lane played a scoreless draw at Central Park before a crowd of 5,000 in the Salter Shield. St Patrick's won the replay. The *Wigan Examiner* reported that,

All conquering Hunslet Carr 1924-5 with the Gilston Cup, Goldthorpe Cup, Hanson Shield, Leeds Cup, Yorkshire Cup. Back Row: Teachers – H. Hobson, G.H. Cripps, J.B. Pickles. Middle Row: L. Johnson, E. Wainwright, C. Bassett, J. Parkes, H. Hinchcliffe, H. Speight. Front Row: H. Taylor, C. Morrell, F. Verity, G. Kirby, T. Gelder, H. Thorpe, W. Wadman. Kneeling: H. Reader

'10,000 was the official attendance but by half-time this had swollen to 15,000'. The team arrived home to, 'scenes of remarkable enthusiasm. They had to walk behind a taxi to reach their charabanc. Crowds lined the streets and The British Legion Band preceded the team up Greenough Street. The crowd fell in behind the coach and marched with pride to Scholes, strains of 'Wearin' o the Green' were belted forth with great gusto, and eye witnesses have stated how there was singing and dancing in the streets as the team arrived home'.

Coalopolis to Pie Eaters,
a celebration of 100 Years of Schools Rugby League in Wigan

We hosted Leigh U16s where I was 'in charge'! The visitors weren't strong and a committed Oldham team were patently too powerful for them. As is often the case when facing classier opponents the Leigh side started to lose heart. With 15 minutes to go they were down to 12 men. After a discussion with the Leigh coach and exhortations from the Oldham lads I decided to play for them in order to make up the numbers. As it was my very first game of rugby I have to say it was a blur and I was grateful to leave the pitch in one piece. Would this happen today? I think not!

Steve Tyrell

I was keen that the kids would realise that it was part of a package of behaving themselves in school, working hard in lessons, and then representing your school was a reward for that in effect. It's no good having somebody that's excellent at rugby league who doesn't show any importance to anything else. The kids who are in teams are ambassadors. All around school we use them as part of the sports council, the kids who get involved in making sure that PE improves. The girls have really embraced it. At first, when we started, girls got it into their head you'd have to be big. They see it now as more being talented and athletic. Some of them like the aggression! Others, the guile of having to try and break down a defence in all sorts of different ways. The stereotype's gone. It's just like most other sports. It's exciting, gives them a confidence. They've already acquired lots of the skills through netball and they like the fact they do get to be a bit physical and they're learning about how to tackle and do things that are quite out the ordinary. It gives them a sense of achievement and they like the success.

George Panayiotou

Mr Cripps left in May 1926 and the boys presented him with a Grandfather clock inscribed, 'in appreciation of his tireless efforts to inspire the boys to play the game in sport and life.'

Hunslet Carr handbook

The winning of the Trophy coming as it did one day before the end of the General Strike, (although the miners did not return to work for a good while afterwards) and in a time of severe depression, was a tonic to the people of the Scholes and Hardybutts area. The game was shown at The Prince's Cinema the following week, giving an indication as to its importance.

The first Daily Dispatch final, 12th May 1926 –
St Patrick's Wigan v St Bede's Widnes

Danby's again were in charge of travel but this time the North Sea crossing to Rotterdam was favoured and the voyage by MV Norland was very pleasant, leaving Hull at 1800 and disembarking 0800 next morning. The excellent dining facilities and unlimited helpings were thoroughly appreciated. However, not all followed the example of one of the boys who changed all his spending money into Belgian

Yorkshire Schools 1950-1.

and not French francs. Set off for the little town of Salon de Provence - welcomed at the nearest Jacques Borel motorway cafe where a souvenir little basket from Provence - sweets, almonds, lavender - presented to the party. Visit to a rather rainy Carcassonne followed by a bit of shopping - most boys took the opportunity of buying a French rugby shirt but K. Jackson picked an extra large size - still scrum halves grow. Montpellier - Accommodation at the local social centre, formerly a seminary. Boys received a souvenir key ring of the city from the Mayor. The tour captain inexplicably lost his passport but due to the efforts of Mr Lee was allowed back in to the country.

France, 1976

Courtney St was a mixed all-age school on Holderness Road in East Hull. It had the reputation as a sporting school, excelling in all but particularly rugby league. It was a two-story building, with girls on the ground floor and boys on the first, always taught separately. It had no playing fields' rugby practice took place on the school playground and sometimes in the corridors. Inter-school matches were played in a local park. The driving force behind the rugby teams was the legendary Stan Adams, who was a strict disciplinarian, in keeping with the regime at the school. Nevertheless his pupils idolised him and still revere his memory because of the time he devoted to them in developing their team. He would have regular practices for them in the last two weeks of the summer holidays in readiness for the coming season. When he marched his team down the streets to games or practice, people would come out of their homes and applaud them as they paraded, military fashion, down the road. Mr Adams was also a rugby league referee, spending his Saturdays officiating professional matches outside the county. There was intense local rivalry with the other schools off Holderness Rd and in the west of the city. The school team only played outside Hull when they were competing in the YSRL U14 cup.

Courtney Street's record in the competition is unsurpassed to this present day. Between 1913/14 and 1947 they reached the final 11 times, winning eight and losing three while there were titanic battles with the likes of Buslingthorpe (Leeds), South Featherstone and Hunslet Carr. During the Second World War, the east of Hull was heavily bombed and many boys were evacuated out of the city. The arrival of a new headmaster in the late forties saw the school switch to soccer. It was eventually closed and demolished during the reparations rebuilding programme.

Tony McGowan, Brian Mathews and Bing Watson, who were at Courtney Street in the late 1930s and early 'Forties

Leeds school Kirkstall Road, Yorkshire Champions after beating Manygates from Wakefield at Belle Vue. Back row: Mr Dacre, Garnett, Stacey, Whitehead, Croll, Walters, Child, Johnson, Page, Mr Dalby. Front row: Harris, Slatcher, Goodall, Turner (capt), Hinch, Stockdill, Child, Lawson.

Little scrum half Carl Dyson lived on Wheldon Lane right opposite the ground. His dad was a very prominent supporter of Cas. You could always hear him wherever he was in the crowd, which earned him the name 'chirrup Dyson'. Carl broke his collar bone and, luckily, Jim Parkin the then Headmaster at Airedale had a car. He took Carl and me to hospital and Carl was strapped up and we took him home. Jim said to me, 'Well Peter lad, here's a bit of experience for you. Go and tell his dad'. I got out and with some trepidation knocked on the front door, which was on the street. Sure enough, his dad came to the door and I said, not too confidently, 'I'm sorry Mr Dyson but your Carl's been playing rugby and he's broken his collar bone'. His dad looked at him and replied, 'Well did tha score a try first?'

Peter Hirst

First time entrants Clare Hall Secondary Modern of Halifax win the YSRL Cup in 1951/2 beating Southdale (Ossett) 18-6 in the final at Crown Flatt, Dewsbury, coached by proud master Jimmy Widdop and including future professional Alan Kellett.

This event, the first of its kind in Runcorn, took place on the Irwell Lane enclosure on Saturday afternoon before 2,000 spectators, the proceeds being given to the National Union of Teachers' Benevolent and Orphan funds. Both teams were the pick of the competitions in their respective towns. The home boys were not to be denied and a round of passing ended in Price planting the leather over the line again. At the conclusion of the match, in the presence of the spectators who gathered round the grandstand, Mr John Littler handed the handsome shield he had presented to the Schoolboys' Competition to W Potter, the captain of the Trinity team. There was a scene of much enthusiasm. Mr Littler, in the course of his speech, dwelt upon the excellent manner in which the competition had been conducted. He urged the boys to take the hard knocks of life with the same toleration and determination they had exhibited

England vice-captain Mike Peers looks to make a break against the French at the Boulevard in 1970.

Cromwell Street, Swinton winners of the '*Evening Chronicle* Shield' in 1956. Back row: Richardson, Bradburn, Cartwright, Cummings (capt), Parker, Hough, Sykes. Front row: Ashden, Daley, Thomas, Hastle, Cunliffe, Saul.

on the field and their life would be brighter and happier than if they lost their tempers and spent their time in useless grumbling. He paid a high compliment to Mr W Shaw, the trainer of the Trinity team, and the officials of the Runcorn Club for their work which had entailed much self-sacrifice. Potter, upon receiving the shield, was hoisted shoulder high amid great cheering. Mr T H Annett said as headmaster of Holy Trinity School he accepted the custody of that shield with pride and pleasure; firstly, because of the giver and secondly because Trinity was the first name inscribed upon it. The two teams, with the school representatives, were afterwards entertained to tea by the Runcorn Club.

Swinton Boys v Runcorn Boys – 6th May 1908

The Bransholme Estate was built in the late 1960s and early 1970s and the first senior comprehensive school opened in

1969 was Bransholme High School. The school system operating in the city was: - Primary 5-10, Junior High 11-14 and Senior High 14-18 (including sixth forms). It meant that Grammar and Secondary modern schools were amalgamated. The posts of Heads of PE invariably went to those from the Grammars and subsequently the main rugby code played at the big comps was rugby union. Bransholme High school fell into this category. As teacher in charge, this was a difficult situation to manage. I came from a Union background, having been signed by HKR from my home town team of Redcar. However, pupils found the transition at 14 very difficult and the vast majority preferred league. There was pressure from parents, governors and councillors at the time for Senior Highs to switch to RL from RU. The success of Bransholme High was down to firstly, the natural ability and passion for the game displayed by the pupils involved; secondly, the tremendous support given by mums, dads and relatives and thirdly, the amazing work done by unpaid volunteers at the Sunday League clubs who helped to coach and develop these young players.

Ged Dunn, Hull KR winger

Many of Warrington's schools (secondary) have been re-organised and a great deal of the history has therefore been lost or misplaced. A lot of the schools that were rugby league orientated, like Bewsey were closed down. Other, such as St Johns and English Martyrs (where John Bevan was head of PE) amalgamated to form Cardinal Newman. Other schools such as Richard Fairclough joined with the Boteler Grammar School where Paul Cullen was educated.

Frank Hawley

'We had nothing like this when I was growing up in London,' said Martin Offiah who was guest of honour and cut the ribbon. 'This is a fantastic facility which will be great for rugby league in the area, both for the clubs who play here and all the schoolkids who are going to use it.' Rob Powell spent four years as a sports development officer based at Archbishop Lanfranc school. Dan Steel, Regional Development Manager (London and South East) commented, 'This is the culmination of a huge amount of work by Archbishop Lanfranc School. We're really pleased to have formed a partnership with such a strong community-based school. The new pitch was in use straight after the launch, with local schools taking part in the Year 8 Carnegie Champion Schools competition.

The official opening of a new floodlit all weather 3G pitch at Archbishop Lanfranc School in Croydon, November 2010.

During a celebration dinner at Dewsbury, at which the principal guests were 18 local schoolboys who were members of the Dewsbury and Batley inter-town rugby team which this season won the Yorkshire Inter-City Schoolboys Rugby League Championship ('B' Division), an outstanding performance by the team captain, David Smith, was referred to by coach, Mr Dennis Evans. David was presented with a miniature cup (given by Mr Jim Brown), as a memento of his performance. He is a pupil at Dewsbury Technical College. Responding to the toast, Coun. J McDonald said the education committee always tried to help the local league by hearing the views of the officials and teachers, and providing playing fields when available. He was proud to have been a player in the inter-town team: 'I attended Batley St Mary's,' he said, 'and have many happy memories of my footballing days'. Mr Harry Smith, proposing the 'Yorkshire County Schools R.L.,' reviewed the growth of the league. I have had some wonderful experiences refereeing and watching the boys play. 'We are hoping next season to provide opportunity for the under

Huddersfield St Patricks U13s team from 1957. Back row (left to right) C. Joyce (reserve), B. Fox, B. Beaumont, F. Hutton, B. Evans, J. Hunt, D.Lockwood (reserve) Front row: J. Regan, G. Chadwick, P. Smith, A. Reilly (capt), J. Wimpenny, M. Starkey, D. Cartledge.

elevens to play rugby. Other districts have already formed an under eleven league and have met with success. Personally I think boys should play as soon as they start school' (Laughter) The donor of the cup, Mr A Sproxton of Hull added, 'Once I was told that rugby was only for mentally deficient people, but although perhaps anyone can put their head down in a pack, the game calls for a nimble wit.' 'Rugby league,' said the speaker, 'was one of the finest games in the world, and one of the many reasons is because women will never play it.' (Laughter) Magic and mystery was later provided by Mr D Lockwood and monologues were given by Mr A O'Keefe.

Newspaper report – 'Local Team's Cup Success' – May 1950

In the first half of the twentieth century the 'all' age of the Boys'/Girls' Schools stood at the very heart of the

Glasshoughton Junior School including Alan Rhodes (front, left) who played for Featherstone Rovers at Wembley.

communities and as such often represented the aspirations of that community when involved in sporting fixtures. It became virtually one community versus another, with fiercely separate religious loyalties. School games often became a meeting of the tribes and attracted huge crowds. Undoubtedly there would have been incidents from time to time, but for the greater part, the game was a unifying common factor.

The demolition of slum housing and the creation of new housing estates broke up the old communities. A better standard of living and the increasing working class awareness of education and technology removed most of the tribal instincts. The organisation today is very different from that which began life in 1967. Much of the competition structure has gone. What does remain is the will to remain faithful to the standards expected of those involved in the activities provided for the boys and girls.

ESRL & its historic roots – Ray Unsworth

Another season is over and done, they seem to move so fast
Another one's about to begin, but with a different cast
For middle schools exist no more, since summer '92
Any many names have disappeared: let's remember just a few
Clapgate Middle won't be engraved, on cups in future years
They sent us the Creassers and Schofield too, and encouraged many players
Armley Middle is in the past, but again they left their mark
As did Belle Isle, Kirsktall also, and who can forget Holt Park?

Intake, Fir Tree, Braim Wood Middles, have all come to a stop
Arthur Greenwood, Royal Park, no 'middle' at John Blenkinsop
Bramley C of E has changed, and Thornhill has totally gone
Hunslet C of E's moved round, so have Greenhill and Halton
We know that rugby was played elsewhere, in primary and in high
But so often it was the middle schools, that made our flag fly high
We must now look to the future, and hope that with the change
Schools and rugby will flourish again, a mixture of old and newer names
Middleton Park, Crawshaw, Woodkirk, they all will still exist
Churwell, Bruntcliffe, Brigshaw, Royds, are others on our list
Teachers, pupils, parents, clubs, must all support each other
So that our sport of rugby league, can rise back and recover
Colin Trenholme - 'An ending ... a beginning ... but no middle'

Since its inception in 2003, the Champion Schools Competition has become firmly embedded in the South of England, with regional festivals taking place in the likes of Richmond and Lambeth, boroughs that are at the opposite end of the social and economic scales of deprivation in London. Brentwood Head of Physical Education, Daniel Iacono said, 'The rise of the profile of the game has been incredible, when I first started at the school only a handful of

The last Hunslet Carr team, winners of the Lewthwaite Trophy. Back row: (left to right) Sissons, Ashley, Hood, Raynor, Henderson. Bottom row: Abbey, Thomson, Walker, Clark, Johnson, Bentley, Ramsey.

students even knew the game existed and no one played, now we have more than 130 students boys and girls who train weekly and who cannot stop talking about teams like the Leeds Rhinos, St Helens, Wigan and Harlequins. Now we find our little school from Essex going to the National Finals, it is really surreal. This tremendous achievement is due to the hard work from the students and the support from all of the staff who give up their time to coach.'

Try-It Brochure

To play a curtain raiser in my day was something different. It was something special. Featherstone played one match in 1967 and it rained. I just went up thinking we'd be playing on the side field at the back and that they wouldn't allow us to go on. Laurie Gant, the coach of Rovers said, 'Send 'em on. Let 'em plough the field up!'

Ken Everson

It is, perhaps, sad that places like Broughton, Preston, Runcorn, Southport, no longer appear in the list of competing towns ... but nevertheless tremendous progress has been made over the past 50 years despite two world wars and the atrocious conditions under which matches have had to be played. In fact it is only since the last war that improvements have, at last, been seen in the way of playing fields and changing accommodation.

The Intermediate inter-town competition began in 1960-62, Leigh defeating Wigan in the Final. The Junior inter-town competition began in 1961-62 season, with Widnes' 11-year-old's giving a superlative display to beat Wigan. That season also saw the beginning of the junior inter school competition where St Patrick's, Wigan added another first, defeating Simm's Cross, Widnes. Lancs-Yorks county matches are acknowledged as producing the cream. One match has been played 'under the lights' - at Bradford in 1955 - though the occasion was marred somewhat by torrential rain and strong winds.

Golden Jubilee Match -
Wigan and District Schoolboys' programme

We have reason to be proud of the sheer weight of numbers of games being played but also, and more importantly, we should be proud of the discipline that is inherent in the schoolboy game, the opportunity that is provided for our boys to experience social occasions organised in a civilised and orderly fashion and the insistence on high moral standards. It is very gratifying to be able to report that not one case of indiscipline was reported during the season and,

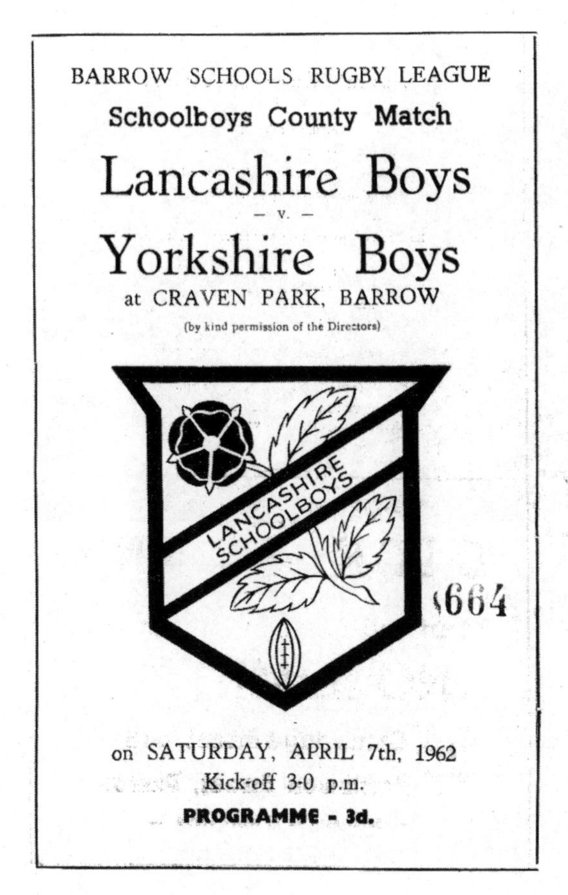
BARROW SCHOOLS RUGBY LEAGUE

Schoolboys County Match

Lancashire Boys

— v. —

Yorkshire Boys

at CRAVEN PARK, BARROW

(by kind permission of the Directors)

on SATURDAY, APRIL 7th, 1962

Kick-off 3-0 p.m.

PROGRAMME - 3d.

Alex Murphy faces Barry Seabourne in a county clash as U15s.

hopefully this is an indication that standards are being maintained. However, in an increasingly violent world, it is well for us to keep a vigilant eye on our sport and each and every case of dismissal, even for a limited period of time, should be reported to this body. Only by being sensitive to this aspect will we continue to keep the schoolboy game as an occasion able to be enjoyed by the tiny but skilful as much as by the large and powerful.

North West Counties - Annual Report 1987-8

Having successfully collected all the party en route to

Hunslet City Boys of 1958 including Bill Ramsey holding the ball and Mick Shoebottom in front of him next to Ray Abbey.

Warrington, onward travel by National coach enabled us to stay overnight near Heathrow. We were honoured there by a visit from the President of the NUM, Mr Joe Gormley, whose grandson was taking part in the tour. He very kindly offered to sponsor our boys for £1 a point scored on tour.

Easter 1980, to France

Although John Gibbs (Thornhill High School) and Peter Tate (West Borough High School) had run some Town Boys sides in the mid seventies it wasn't until the summer of 1977 that the association was officially reformed. A meeting was held at the Shoulder of Mutton, Halifax Road. Five teachers attended - John Gibbs, Peter Tate, Martin Crick (St John Fisher RC High School) John Spencer (Hightown C of E Junior School) and Howard Widmore (Wellhouse Middle School). The association carried the Dewsbury and Batley banner but schools from Cleckheaton, Heckmondwike,

Liversedge and Mirfield would be involved. Woodkirk High from Tingley also joined. Growth was slow at first. Inter School cup competitions were introduced from U11 through to U16. The finals for these events were held at Mount Pleasant and Crown Flatt. Eventually incorporated into a day of rugby, when all six finals were staged on May Day Bank Holiday Monday, it often attracted a crowd near four figures. The Club and Institute in Dewsbury at the back of Marks and Spencer's became the venue for meetings for the next eight years. In the mid eighties the meetings moved to the Gate pub. Landlord Dave Foster was a former Batley player whose son, Michael, played at Wembley in the 1983 curtain raiser.

John Spencer - Heavy Woollen reformation

I came as Head of PE to the Boys Modern. The standard of the boys coming in at 11 was phenomenal. They watched the professionals play but they were also in teams at school from age seven. I had Mick Redfearn in the centre. Playing against him was the guy who played alongside him in the Castleford and also the county side, Wilf Newton. They were knocking seven bells out of each other. In the end, Roy did the first sin binning I've ever seen on a rugby field and that was years before it had ever been thought of for rugby league. He sent Mick over to me and said: 'You go stand on that touchline.' He said to Wilf Newton: 'You go stand on that touchline. And you're off for ten minutes. After ten minutes I'll bring you back on. If you carry on like that, you'll be off for good.' It calmed them down and I thought that was a great move. But, you could do that as a teacher in those days.

I always had a principle that it was sport and you played it the right way, 'robust but clean.' I always had a theory that if you got the wrong side of the referee and he was penalising you, then forever you were getting kicked back. Your job wasn't to run a rugby team and to win all the games, it was to teach the boys something about how to conduct themselves on a field. Children now live a different life. Lads in Castleford didn't go very far. They didn't go on foreign holidays. Their life was rugby. They wanted to play rugby. They wanted to watch rugby. They were interested in rugby. It was the highlight of their life. Never mind school and lessons ... in the heyday it was the school team or nothing.

Danny Stephens and myself were very good friends. We'd socialise together but we had a disagreement about refereeing. My boys didn't always agree with the way I refereed, because if we were playing a team that were not as good as us, then perhaps wrongly, I'd even it up a bit. I always thought it was good for them to play under the pressure of knowing that they couldn't make the slightest mistake or be pulled up. You've got to learn to cope with that. Danny never agreed. He always said, 'No, you referee exactly - every decision got to be spot on'. But refereeing schoolboys you've got to just adapt a little.

Peter Dawson

Normanton has a long tradition of families. A lot of their brothers, uncles, cousins, fathers have all gone through and played for Freeston. It's a production line. On a Friday night, I would guarantee that 99% of these kids will be sitting at home watching Super League with their dads and their families. If you go to a game at Normanton, you play with 500 people on the sideline. You've got half the school out and all the parents and others in the town come to watch it. People don't like coming here. They call it 'the fortress'. When the bell goes at 2.35, if there's any age group game on, you'll have the rugby teams and people in that year watching. The girls' rugby has grown. They're saying, 'We'll play, we can do it.'

Lee Hudson

3

*

Rivalries

In 1970-71 Bewsey had a bit of a rough reputation. Just before the semi-final of the Champion Schools Cup v Stockton Heath, our coach Malcolm Knowlden told our lads to pay particular concern to their best player Dave Sutton. Dave was from Walton Village and made Prince Charles sound like Arthur Mullard, very posh. But boy was he a tough nut. Our lads battered him from start to finish but he held out and got their one try.

The next day three of our lads were told to go to Mr Knowlden's office where, due to the unduly rough play they would get three of the best, and 'Knocker' told them to bend over for the stick. Mike Peers said that if he got the stick he wouldn't play again for the school. Mr Knowlden thought about it for a few seconds and, realising Peers was the best player, decided on another outcome. He told Peers to cry out as if in pain and each time he hit the desk with the stick so as not to give the game away to the other two outside.

Tommy Griffiths

The game that was to influence my life took place in late 1961 at Merton Bank playing fields between St Helens and Wigan. I was greatly surprised for two reason; one was the number of people on the touchline waiting for the start; there must have been at least a thousand with many more

Cumberland Schools U16s 1961-2.

arriving during the course of the first half, and how vociferous and full of fervour the crowd was. It was just like being at a Wigan Saints professional game, albeit on a smaller scale. The second surprise was the attitude of the teachers on the touchline.

I knew a number of the St Helens' teachers and was amazed to see people whom I knew to be rational, calm professionals whilst doing their day jobs, lose all sense of rationality and impartiality as soon as the game started. Yes I was surprised, but over the years I became exactly like them!

Jim Forshaw – who served for many years as
Treasurer of North West Counties and was
Chairman of English Schools' Rugby League from 1992-94.

Rivalry next year will be keen not only for the existing trophies, including the Richard Part trophy, awarded to the SSYCARLA Player of the Year, which was this year won by Tony Farquhar (McEntee Senior High School, Walthamstow) but also for the new competitions, among them the Daneford P.T.A. R.L. Challenge Cup.

Southern Schools and Youth Clubs
Amateur Rugby League Association newsletter

I had begun teaching at Saddleworth which at the time was expanding from a small village school into a large comprehensive. A year later Saddleworth School included rugby league in the curriculum. I had become used to the inter school rivalry in the many other sports but rugby league was far more intense.

Fred Laughton ran rugby at St Albans and was a hard working enthusiast still remembered with deep affection in the town. Laurie Kearns of Oldham Tinkers fame ran league at St Anselms and always tempered his passion for the sport with dry humour which invariably put things in perspective. Iain MacCorquodale began rugby league at Fitton Hill which he saw as both a means of channelling aggression and giving youth an opportunity of achieving success.

He did a marvellous job. Derek Wild a self confessed karate addict made sure that trips to Counthill School were spicy and when Eric Fitzsimons kicked off the sport at Failsworth School and Dave Fricker extended the work done by Ged Sweeney at Breezehill, league really took off in the town.

Former Great Britain coach Phil Larder

Because our Head of Sport, George Cranage, hailed from the Hunslet area - having built Yorkshire Cup winning teams at Belle Isle - we found ourselves training with Hunslet schools.

You may not think that where we played our representative rugby mattered to us, after all we had only just begun playing anything that resembled structured rugby. But, there was the small matter of the River Aire and we lived on the Leeds side of it. Despite the same terraced streets and the same red brick factories, the same smoke and the same fumes, crossing the river and venturing into deepest Hunslet was like travelling into a foreign land.

Nevertheless we went and trained, because we dare not do otherwise and must have impressed for a number of us found ourselves in the Hunslet Boys team to play Huddersfield at the Arthur Thornton ground.

Philip Haller, who played in the first-ever schoolboys Test v France

From the High School days we had a hooker called John McNeill. He was one for the quip was Tosh. We'd gone to

YORKSHIRE SCHOOLS RUGBY LEAGUE

YORKSHIRE

VERSUS

LANCASHIRE

AT WHELDON ROAD, CASTLEFORD

(by kind permission of CASTLEFORD R.L.F.C.)

SATURDAY, DEC. 4th, 1965

KICK—OFF 2-30 P.M.

Souvenir Programme - 6d each

33, Wynne Road,
St. Helens.

Dear Tom,
Congratulations on your being chosen for the England party! It is unfortunate that you must miss your chance of a Lancashire Cup medal, but these things happen.
Good luck and best wishes,
R. Middlehurst.

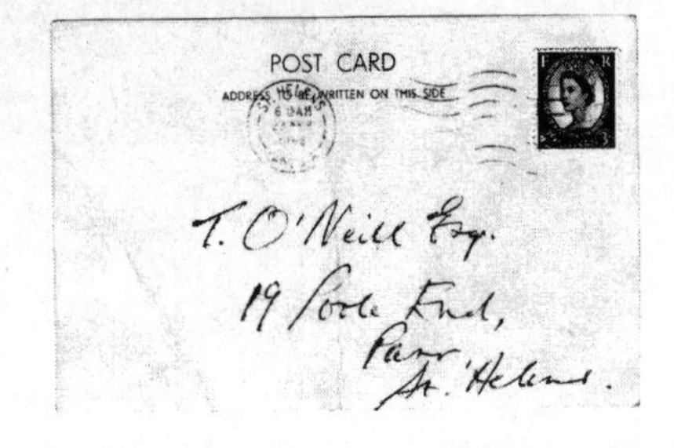

POST CARD
ADDRESS TO BE WRITTEN ON THIS SIDE

T. O'Neill Esq.
19 Poole End,
Parr
St. Helens.

play at Normanton. We're walking out to the pitch and he was with his opposite number and had a ball in his hands. This is when they had to fight for the ball, contested scrums, and he said, 'Here old lad, have a look at that cos that's last tha'll see of it all day!'

Peter Hirst

This first Independent Schools Ten-a-side rugby league festival represents another breakthrough. Five schools may not seem to be terribly significant, but the fact that these high-powered educational institutions have included rugby league in their summer term sporting programme indicates the higher profile which the game now commands.

There may be a shortage of rugby league experience in today's teams, but there will be no shortage of enthusiasm, skill and athleticism.

Steve Alderson, Secretary BUSCARLA, programme notes

I was selected as vice captain of England Schoolboys against France at the Boulevard. My parents and girlfriend attended and as usual with the French lads it was a very physical game.

It was the first time my mum had ever watched me play and early in the second half a massive brawl took place on the touchline where they were standing. Myself and a French prop were swapping punches and finished up hanging over the wall.

I spotted my mother running down the terraces with her umbrella waving. She proceeded to batter the poor French prop shouting leave him alone. That's my little lad. It was revealed after the prop had two cracked ribs and it cost me dad a fiver for a new umbrella. She only ever watched me one more time. A Lancashire Shield Final at Central Park - I was sent off after seven minutes. My dad banned her from going after that.

Mike Peers

The Southern Schools and Youth Clubs Amateur Rugby League Association was formed in February, 1978. We have been greatly assisted by touring teams from the north and from our fellow-pioneers in Scotland.

Prominent R.L. players have always been on hand to come down South and help promote the game. We are certainly developing the game in the South but against tremendous odds. If our boys are to reach a high standard, they first of all need regular matches against northern opposition.

Dave Part

In 1974 a challenge match was arranged as a curtain-raiser to the Championship Final at Central Park between the Lancashire Shield Winners and their Yorkshire counterparts. The two teams involved were St John Fisher, Wigan and Cross Green Comprehensive, Leeds. The game ended with a victory for Fisher by 42 points to 10. In September 1980, the Executive of English Schools' Rugby League instituted a new competition.

Four teams from Lancashire and four from Yorkshire would compete in a knock-out to determine the premier team in the country. North-West Counties S.R.L. nominated the four semi-finalists from the '*Evening News*' Shield Competition, whereas East of Pennines S.R.L. selected the four teams which they considered the best in their region.

The road to Champion Schools

I remember going up to see Matt Cook and Desi Williams play in the Yorkshire v North West trial game at Castleford. The town team system was the representative one of that period that enabled southern-based players to be exposed to other levels of rugby and it started the ongoing trend of them gaining national honours.

Under the town team format from 1998-2000 there was ourselves, North London and Hemel Hempstead. Our team played in the Broncos kit and the home venue for school games was Marble Hill Park.

South Wales had a team in as well. Then we would get through to play a 'northern' team. I do remember taking a side to play Featherstone. We competed quite well but got taken apart on occasions by a tiny bloke - Rob Burrow!

The cheery young faces of St Albans, Warrington.

Our first rep honours came with Bobby Wallis - who played for Yorkshire. He was due to play for English Schools but during an innocuous passing of a ball, not in a game, he tore ligaments in his knee and had to withdraw.

Joe Mbu was the first to make it to English Schools. He went on tour, and the feedback was that he was invaluable as a player but also as a translator as he was fluent in French!

Graeme Thompson, former development officer and Scotland international now on RL European Federation Board

Through the 1960s, Saturdays were spent travelling across the Pennines on the old 'A' roads. These matches would end with formal meals (often in schools) with speeches. Boys were expected to travel in school uniform. Afterwards they would attend the professional game. A seven-a-side tournament began, which was held on the last Saturday before schools broke up for Easter on the vast fields of Snapethorpe Secondary Modern.

In the 70s, matches would take place after school as travelling was much easier and high schools in particular had their own mini buses. A strong U11 section developed and an added attraction was the Les Pounder Trophy, donated by the chairman of Wakefield Trinity and played for at half time during Trinity home matches by teams of 9-a-side. District matches meant regular cross-Pennine travel on the M62 played in a morning usually on school fields with light refreshments provided. Return would be after the games and all were back by early afternoon.

During the 70s and 80s Wakefield Schools finals were always held at Belle Vue and financial support was forthcoming from a third of the takings of a gate that the schools manned and provided the funds from which the association could help schools with kit grants etc. This was only stopped in the late 1980s by the tax man wanting his cut.

In the 1990s the number of schools playing was declining as teachers were having to spend more time elsewhere in education and could afford little time for extra curricular activities. Wakefield schools also lost a great servant of over 30 years in Tony Profitt as did Yorkshire schools where he was a life member and ESRL where he was treasurer for many years.

In 1993 Wakefield Metropolitan District need to unify its schools and the middle schools were closed. High schools became 11-16 or 11-18 and junior and infant schools formed. Names like Manygates who had played through the decades disappeared because at the time competitive sport was frowned upon in junior schools so no rugby was played except for tag sessions run by Wakefield Trinity.

Wakefield schools and Castleford schools did join together for financial purposes so that a sports grant from the Wakefield Metropolitan Schools Sports Federation could be claimed. This duly done they then halved it and played separate teams.

Girls rugby league has been a major development. Now 16 of the district's 20 high schools play some rugby league.

Bernie Smith

I hope your crusade is still going well in the London schools amongst the Southern heathens. I was delighted to know how many schools were now playing the game and it is obvious to me that the B.B.C. showing matches, such as last night's floodlit cup final between St. Helens and Widnes, must do you the power of good.

Jim Johnson, M.P.

Exactly one hundred years after Batley had beaten St Helens at Headingley in the very first Challenge Cup final, Batley and Dewsbury Schools played St Helens in the curtain raiser. To add nostalgia to the occasion both teams wore copies of the kit from 1897. As a result of a security alert the game was reduced to seven minutes each way.

Tony Rhodes, the secretary of Batley and Dewsbury Schools recalls, 'We had to wait outside while the stadium was checked. Nobody knew whether the game would go ahead, David Howes re-organised the timetable and shortened the game. It was a bit of a rush in the changing rooms and coach John Drake found that some of the bigger boys couldn't fit into their kit and some of them actually played in different numbered jerseys.'

Wembley curtain raiser, 1977

We had a strong team which throughout the four years of high school only lost a handful of games at both league and union.

I was captain of the teams in both codes and as U15s we had our finest achievement in league when we beat Outwood Grange (led by former Leeds and Wakefield halfback Mark Conway) in the Yorkshire Schools cup final at Post Office Road.

Our greatest disappointment was undoubtedly the following year when we were dumped out of the Yorkshire Cup by a Lee Crooks inspired Sydney Smith's School in Hull. Lee played scrum half in this game and almost single-handedly guided them to victory.

Top referee Russell Smith

The Huddersfield Town Team of 1963.

We went up to Airedale High and at the time they didn't play rugby league. In the fifth year we got together and asked one of the English teachers, Steve Ridders, if he would enter us for the Yorkshire Cup competition. We told him as long as he would do the admin work, we'd train ourselves. He did and, sure enough, we won it. The school's played rugby league since and produced a lot of great players, like Joe Westerman and Rob Burrow.

Bob Beardmore, Castleford scrum half

Rugby league continues to flourish and is growing in Walton-on-Thames and beyond. It is still based at Ambleside Avenue but due to the new appointments of two of their former schoolteachers the game has been started at Spring

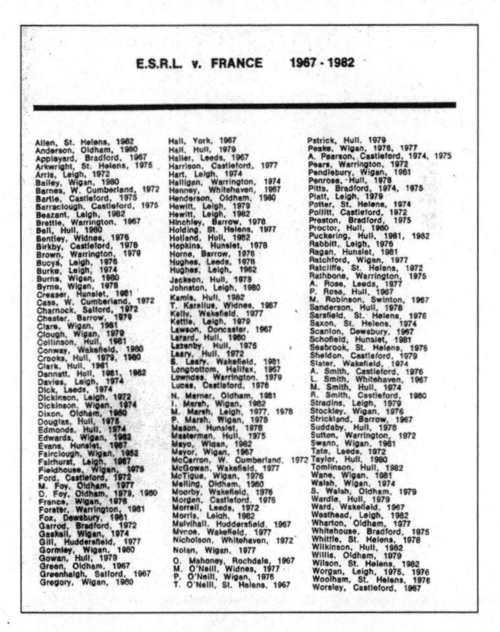

E.S.R.L. v. FRANCE 1967 - 1982

Allen, St. Helens, 1982
Anderson, Oldham, 1980
Appleyard, Bradford, 1967
Arkwright, St. Helens, 1975
Arris, Leigh, 1972
Bailey, Wigan, 1980
Barnes, W. Cumberland, 1972
Bartle, Castleford, 1975
Barraclough, Castleford, 1975
Beazant, Leigh, 1982
Brettle, Warrington, 1967
Bell, Hull, 1980
Bentley, Widnes, 1976
Birkby, Castleford, 1978
Brown, Warrington, 1979
Bucys, Leigh, 1976
Burke, Leigh, 1974
Burns, Wigan, 1980
Byrne, Wigan, 1978
Creaser, Hunslet, 1981
Cass, W. Cumberland, 1972
Charnock, Salford, 1972
Chester, Barrow, 1979
Clare, Wigan, 1981
Clough, Wigan, 1979
Collinson, Hull, 1981
Conway, Wakefield, 1980
Crooks, Hull, 1979, 1980
Clark, Hull, 1981
Dannatt, Hull, 1981, 1982
Davies, Leigh, 1974
Dick, Leeds, 1974
Dickinson, Leigh, 1972
Dickinson, Wigan, 1974
Dixon, Oldham, 1980
Douglas, Hull, 1975
Edmonds, Hull, 1974
Edwards, Wigan, 1982
Evans, Hunslet, 1967
Fairclough, Wigan, 1982
Fairhurst, Leigh, 1967
Fieldhouse, Wigan, 1976
Ford, Castleford, 1972
M. Foy, Oldham, 1977
D. Foy, Oldham, 1979, 1980
France, Wigan, 1976
Forster, Warrington, 1981
Fox, Dewsbury, 1981
Garrod, Bradford, 1972
Gaskell, Wigan, 1974
Gill, Huddersfield, 1977
Gormley, Wigan, 1980
Gowan, Hull, 1979
Green, Oldham, 1967
Greenhalgh, Salford, 1967
Gregory, Wigan, 1980
Hall, York, 1967
Hall, Hull, 1979
Haller, Leeds, 1967
Harrison, Castleford, 1977
Hart, Leigh, 1974
Halligan, Warrington, 1974
Henney, Whitehaven, 1967
Henderson, Oldham, 1980
Hewitt, Leigh, 1979
Hewitt, Leigh, 1982
Hinchley, Barrow, 1978
Holding, St. Helens, 1977
Holland, Hull, 1982
Hopkins, Hunslet, 1978
Horne, Barrow, 1976
Hughes, Leeds, 1978
Hughes, Leigh, 1982
Jackson, Hull, 1978
Johnston, Leigh, 1980
Kamis, Hull, 1982
T. Karalius, Widnes, 1967
Kelly, Wakefield, 1977
Kettle, Leigh, 1979
Lawson, Doncaster, 1967
Larard, Hull, 1980
Lazenby, Hull, 1975
Leary, Hull, 1972
S. Leary, Wakefield, 1981
Longbottom, Halifax, 1967
Lowndes, Warrington, 1979
Lucas, Castleford, 1976
N. Marner, Oldham, 1981
I. Marsh, Wigan, 1982
M. Marsh, Leigh, 1977, 1978
P. Marsh, Wigan, 1978
Mason, Hunslet, 1978
Masterman, Hull, 1975
Mayo, Wigan, 1982
Mayor, Wigan, 1967
McCarron, W. Cumberland, 1972
McGowan, Wakefield, 1977
McTigue, Wigan, 1976
Melling, Oldham, 1980
Moorby, Wakefield, 1976
Morgan, Castleford, 1976
Morrell, Leeds, 1972
Morris, Leigh, 1982
Mulvihall, Huddersfield, 1967
Mycoe, Wakefield, 1977
Nicholson, Whitehaven, 1972
Nolan, Wigan, 1977
O. Mahoney, Rochdale, 1967
M. O'Neill, Widnes, 1977
P. O'Neill, Wigan, 1976
T. O'Neill, St. Helens, 1967
Patrick, Hull, 1979
Peake, Wigan, 1976, 1977
A. Pearson, Castleford, 1974, 1975
Pears, Warrington, 1972
Pendlebury, Wigan, 1981
Penrose, Hull, 1978
Pitts, Bradford, 1974, 1975
Platt, Leigh, 1979
Potter, St. Helens, 1974
Pollitt, Castleford, 1972
Preston, Bradford, 1975
Proctor, Hull, 1980
Puckering, Hull, 1981, 1982
Rabbitt, Leigh, 1976
Ragan, Hunslet, 1981
Ratchford, Wigan, 1977
Ratcliffe, St. Helens, 1972
Rathbone, Warrington, 1975
A. Rose, Leeds, 1977
P. Rose, Hull, 1967
M. Robinson, Swinton, 1967
Sanderson, Hull, 1978
Sarsfield, St. Helens, 1976
Saxon, St. Helens, 1974
Scanlon, Dewsbury, 1967
Schofield, Hunslet, 1981
Seabrook, St. Helens, 1976
Sheldon, Castleford, 1979
Slater, Wakefield, 1974
A. Smith, Castleford, 1976
L. Smith, Whitehaven, 1967
M. Smith, Hull, 1974
R. Smith, Castleford, 1980
Stradins, Leigh, 1979
Stockley, Wigan, 1976
Strickland, Barrow, 1967
Suddaby, Hull, 1978
Sutton, Warrington, 1972
Swann, Wigan, 1981
Tate, Leeds, 1972
Taylor, Hull, 1980
Tomlinson, Hull, 1982
Wane, Wigan, 1981
Walsh, Wigan, 1974
S. Walsh, Oldham, 1979
Wardle, Hull, 1979
Ward, Wakefield, 1967
Westhead, Leigh, 1982
Wharton, Oldham, 1977
Whitehouse, Bradford, 1975
Whittle, St. Helens, 1978
Wilkinson, Hull, 1982
Willis, Oldham, 1979
Wilson, St. Helens, 1982
Worgan, Leigh, 1975, 1976
Woolham, St. Helens, 1976
Worsley, Castleford, 1967

Taken from the back of a 1983 international programme against France held at Wigan's Central Park.

MENU

✻

Cream of Chicken Soup

✻

Poached Halibut,
Tomato & White Sauce.

✻

Roast Sirloin of Beef,
Horseradish Sauce,
Chopped Ham &
Stuffed Tomatoes,
Roast Potatoes,
Buttered Peas,
Diced Carrots.

✻

Meringue &
Neapolitan Ice Cream,
Melba Sauce,
Whipped Cream.

✻

Cheese & Biscuits

✻

Coffee

Menu, running order for Yorkshire v Lancashire Boys, Saturday March 27th 1965 reception held at the De Grey Rooms, York.

Welcome:

K. E. HUMPHREYS

Chairman of Yorkshire Schools' Rugby League

Our Guests:

Proposed by:

G. R. CHESTER

President of Yorkshire Schools' Rugby League

Reply by:

F. HOWARTH B. A.

Chairman of Lancashire Schools' Rugby League

Presentation of Badges:

The Rt. Hon. The Lord Mayor of York

Clr. S. PALPHRAMAND J. P.

Vote of Thanks:

Proposed by:

B. HALL

Vice - Chairman of Yorkshire Schools' Rugby League

Seconded by:

A. E. CAUSEY

Vice - Chairman of Lancashire Schools' Rugby League

Joe Manley, who refereed the 1965 Challenge Cup final between Hunslet and Wigan, and was deputy head teacher at Orford Secondary Modern , Warrington is applauded on to the field.

Grove Junior School in Hounslow and at the Godalming Middle School even further into the Surrey countryside. St Thomas the Apostle School in Chertsey also intend to play regularly.

We now feel the area is strong enough to run a league and possibly a cup competition at U12 and U11 age groups.

Report of London Schools Rugby League in late 1970s

The City Boys team was to play Wigan Boys in what was an unofficial championship decider as both teams were undefeated on their side of the Pennines. We arrived at the allotted venue by coach after an early start from Leeds and

George Street Juniors 1962. Back row (left to right) Richard Davis, John Price, Jim Roberts, Jeff Carter, Steve Hankins, Rob Walker, Mal Anders. Front row (left to right) Barry Evans, Terry Sykes, Pete Goldsborough, Billy Telford, Dave Fisher, Steve Northern, Keith Bell.

were ready and eager to play when the bus was boarded by a Wigan official, who shouted to the lads down the coach, "Bet you'd rather play at Central Park as a curtain raiser to the Wigan Leeds game wouldn't you?" You can imagine the response.

"It'll just mean a slight alteration to the scheduled arrangements," he explained.

"Instead of having something to eat after the game we've got something laid on now," he smiled. The coach drew into a school playground not far away and we got out expecting one or two curled up sandwiches and if we were lucky a greasy sausage roll. We walked into a school hall that had been transformed into what appeared to be a banqueting suite. Steak and kidney pie, chips, peas and gravy followed by trifle plus all the trimmings were placed in front of us.

"Go easy on the chips lads." Implored our teachers – but to no avail.

My mate, who was playing hooker, shifted more chips than anybody I've ever seen before (or since) in one sitting. I couldn't work out where it was all going until we packed down for the first scrum later on. I was open side prop and he was usually light as a feather to hold up, but that afternoon – I had more trouble with him in the pack, than I had with my opposite number.

Needless to say we lost the game by a comfortable margin and in the report in the following week's Green Final it said, "Leeds' forwards were ineffective and their backs pedestrian." To this day I still don't know if it was South West Lancashire hospitality, or a touch of gamesmanship.

Philip Haller

4

*

Making Do

Our training ground at St Joseph's was the school brow (pronounced brew) an area of dirt in summer and mud in winter; full of glass, refuse and adjacent to the canal, so no kicking. I and most of my colleagues suffered from infected cuts for many years.

We had two coaches, Mr Kane, Deputy Headteacher and Mr Unsworth took us to the final of the Platt Cup, having beaten St Edward's in the semi final on Gallagher's Field. It was a 'field' with no grass, had an ever present smell from the adjacent bone-works and, with Mr Kane refereeing in his suit, we had at least a try start in every match. We played St William's in the final and despite our subtle plan in having oranges at half-time, we lost. Mind you there was grass on the pitch; we had no chance.

Peter Phillips,
Head teacher St Edmund Arrowsmith High School

Consider the situation in the early 1900s. There would be little if any access to telephones; in a Lancashire Schools' Handbook of 1938 there was not one single telephone number given for any of the Officials or members of the Executive. So recourse was to corresponding by hand-written letters. That is of course after initial contacts have been made with like-minded persons, a long process. Public transport was not as available. Games between schools involved a good degree of walking, despite distance involved. The staging of Representative games follows only when structures are in place; regular competition, good administration and a unity of purpose. The bringing together of boys from different schools; selecting the players and then merging them into one team, take time. There are also the privations and conditions of the times. It is not likely that the schoolboy possessed proper boots. The provision of playing kit would probably have depended upon sponsorship in a time of minimal communication. The efforts of the early schoolteachers are almost homeric in both effort and achievement. George Millard, who taught at Pemberton Colliery School is synonymous with those early years. In 1963 he was an honoured guest at the Jubilee County game between Lancashire and Yorkshire Schools which was staged at Central Park. He must have been very proud that the pioneering work he and his colleagues undertook had flowered to such a rich bloom.

Ray Unsworth, Secretary ESRL

First of all I had nothing to do with sports, people left and in the end they said, 'Will you do it?' It was quite a job, we used to use Leeds Corporation transport, we had vouchers to take the kids and sometimes it was very difficult getting sixteen boys on the bus all at once. I never did have any trouble with the rugby league lads.

Ken Breach

In the late 1980s there was much debate about the use of protective clothing especially shoulder pads in rugby league. BARLA made a decision to allow junior players to wear them but English Schools did not. My clearest memory is of an U13 game in 1993 when York Schools Under 13s

South Featherstone Seniors, 1968-9. Back row (left to right) Kev Barker, Nigel Walton, Ron Derrick, Doug Firth, Keith Brear, Gary Downs, Chris Marsh, Jeff Strut. Sitting (left to right) Dave Carter, Bill Luckman, Derrick Hill, Keith Bell, Gordon Hankins, Steve Coulson, Alan Harrap. Floor: Rob Woodhead (left), Rob Longley.

Warrington Intermediates, winners of the Lancashire Cup in 1969 beating Oldham at the Watersheddings 6-3. Back row (right to left) Savage, Carr, Hayes, Waterman, Holbrook, Stott, Callister, G. Aston, Flood. Middle row (right to left) Crawford, Siddle, Hill, Peers (capt), D. Aston, Danials, Spencer. Front: Claffy, Holbrook.

visited Halifax schools. A twelve year old scrum half took the field wearing his shoulder pads which he wore for all his games when playing for Lock Lane Juniors. It was an unwritten rule that as long as both sides agreed, then pads could be worn despite no official ruling. However, in this case no such agreement had been discussed and the boy concerned was politely asked to remove them. His father, a former RL professional with Sheffield Eagles and York, was not happy but agreed to comply. After about ten minutes the lad went down in a tackle. It was clear that he had a shoulder injury. As his coach, I attended him and carried him from the field. It was quite clear that he had a suspected broken collar bone. As a result I was determined to get a change to the rules. I tabled a motion. There was some debate. It was felt that some boys would gain an unfair advantage and be physically intimidating. Also that this equipment would give boys a false sense of safety and might make them undertake dangerous tackles. The traditionalists mounted fierce opposition and the motion was soundly defeated at the English Schools AGM of 1994. However, with the support of the Hull Schools Association, I continued. During the next year at meetings and matches efforts were made to persuade people and that it was incongruous to have double standards. The matter was tabled again in 1996 where it was passed. The young scrum half was Gareth Ellis.

Dave Milburn

I'd be 13, the war had more or less finished. Nobody had got anything, so the first set of jerseys we ever got were all different colours. The girls in the sewing class made all the shorts out of blackout curtains. You used to get your own boots. I hadn't a pair but my uncle had and they fit me so he gave me his to play in. It was what we could scrounge. The last game we played before I left, I think we got a set of jerseys. I wouldn't have dreamed of girls playing rugby. I think my granddaughter wanted to play because her mates play. You're in with the team aren't you? If you're not, you're out. She must have enjoyed it as she played with two broken fingers.

Brian Nettleton

Attending St Alban's Primary School in the centre of the town meant that the nearest we got to doing PE was a weekly visit to the local baths and a far less frequent visit to the town's (then) only gymnasium in Palmyra Square. There was no grass to be seen. The boys in my class and the year group below were sports mad and we persuaded Sr. Marie Louise, the head teacher, to allow us to form a rugby team. Mike Cooper's dad, a local butcher, provided the kit. The

The inaugural ESRL tour to France in '67, Barrow Schools' Bill Strickland in possession.

team was captained by the late Billy 'Wizzer' Cowell who later signed for Warrington and, after his playing career ended, was often to be seen on the pitch as what was then called the 'sponge man'. Billy and I were given permission to visit St Mary's and ask Miss Kilburn whether or not we could play on Saturday morning at Victoria Park. Permission granted the team duly turned up only to find that we had to somehow clear all of the pink foam that had been created by the chemicals from the local soap-works being whipped up by the weir. I qualified as a teacher in 1972 and took up a position at St John's Catholic Secondary Modern School in Latchford where rugby league had been well established. The school was very small with an annual intake of about sixty pupils, boys and girls. This meant that running a rugby team was nigh on impossible but the enthusiasm from the pupils, the support of the head of PE (John Rigby) and from other PE staff in the town not only made it possible but most enjoyable as well. We played a 'staff v students Y11' game at Easter and can remember Carl Webb, who was then only 14 (but was so good he was allowed to play with the senior boys) pick me up and dump me head first into the very hard turf.

Frank Hawley

In those days there were no parents that could pack half a dozen kids in the car. We just went. At South Featherstone School there were some sinks, so if you came in from the game splattered up to the eyeballs, you could just manage to wash. Then you went home in all your muck! The pitch at the back of the school was quite a small one. It had been re-sown and so the boss wouldn't let us play on it for a couple of years until it got well established. So, we used to walk down to Purston Park. One of the lads hurt his leg and there was no transport down there. A couple of spectators on the

The inaugural England squad strike a pose in Perpignan.

touchline got a bicycle and wheeled him back to school. When I got there, he was in hospital with a broken thigh! Nowadays I'd be out of my job immediately. There was no health and safety, no such thing as insurance, no comebacks from anybody. There was no headteacher saying, 'be careful of this or that.' He was as keen as I was. It wasn't being irresponsible and I'm sure that sport made them more rounded people, they adapted to school with a good spirit because they'd got lessons they'd put up with for part of the day and then rugby later which was a bit special. In one game I awarded a penalty. The kick was straight but it was falling short. One of the opposition team jumped up, two hands in the air, to catch it. But, in doing so, it bounced off his hands and over the crossbar! Is that two points or not? I gave it after consultation with their teacher. It still worries me.

Ken Buck

Prior to the first-ever Test, the visiting side are introduced to the French Minister of Education and then exchange pennants.

We had two strips. A black and white hooped strip and a red and white hooped strip. If you were lucky and had games lessons on a Monday, it was all clean and dry and washed and tidy. If you had it on a Friday, everybody had worn it all week but we never worried about it. If you talk to a lot of people who have achieved in their lives you'll find someone who was instrumental in encouraging them and 99% of them are a teacher.

Bill Clift

I noticed they were a very skilful set and were always playing rugby.

It was touch and pass in a concrete yard.

There were one or two windows broken but nothing was done about that because it was the only area they had. In Burmantofts, I used to get the kids on the bus and then we went to Soldiers Field and played our matches there.

At the end, this chap came across to me - I can see him now with a polo neck jersey on - and said, 'I'd like to congratulate you on the way those lads played rugby!'

I said, 'Oh, thank you very much. That's very nice.'

He said, 'You don't know who I am do you?'

I said, 'No, I'm sorry. I don't.'

He said, 'I'm Eddie Waring of the *Sunday Pictorial.*'

I got as much joy and satisfaction out of seeing kids who I knew weren't going to become professionals but who'd improve their skill, enjoyed the game, could participate and even if I said, 'Here, you referee for a while!'

They'd do it. Everybody at the school realised that rugby was important.

It was the core of the school in a way.

Roy Close

In 1973, the playing fields of our new school became in use. Unfortunately the pitch was too small. To prevent the ball going into the brook and sailing down to the Mersey, all goal kicks were taken from the other end.

G.E.Bannon – Headmaster Sacred Heart Primary

Goal-kicking prop Philip Haller, chosen by Leeds Schools as the representative on their first tour to France in 1967.

ENGLISH SCHOOLS RUGBY LEAGUE

La Tintelee,
Low Moresby,
Whitehaven, CA28 6RT.

10th December, 1975

Dear Colleague,

At an Executive Meeting held on 5.12.75 the following matters were discussed:

1) Humberside, as an Associate County, was granted a none voting observer at E.S.R.L. Executive meetings.

2) Certain items in the BARLA Constitution would appear to conflict with the autonomy of E.S.R.L. BARLA is to be asked to reconsider these items.

3) An E.S.R.L. party will visit France for a Rugby playing holiday, between March 21st and 29th. The party will consist of 32 boys who will be nominated by East of Pennines and West of Pennines, and who will meet for squad practices in late January - early February.

4) Mr. P.B. Latham, Chairman of E.S.R.L. has been nominated for the office of Vice Chairman of the National Council for School Sports.

5) To date a total of 80 National League games (at U16 and U13) out of a total of 82 possible games have been played. All concerned are congratulated upon this achievement.

6) A draft copy of the proposed Amendment to the Constitution of E.S.R.L. is enclosed for your attention. PLEASE IGNORE SIDE TWO, SHEET ONE. You are asked to forward any comments you may have on this to me before January 31st.

7) E.S.R.L. will provide a curtain raiser to the 1976 Cup Final upon similar lines to the 1975 game. Sides to take part will be announced later.

8) The promised grant of £12,000 from R.F.L. has not yet materialised.

9) Howard Firth, formerly of Humberside, has introduced Rugby League Football to his School at West Denton High School, West Denton, Newcastle upon Tyne, and would welcome fixtures with Schools within easy travelling distances of Newcastle. Schools interested in this venture, especially in York, Leeds area, Northern Humberside and Cumbria are asked to contact Mr. Firth, who is willing to travel.

Yours sincerely,

Hard on the heels of this educational upheaval, came the reorganisation of local government. Hardest hit here was Lancashire, losing Barrow to Cumbria, Warrington and Widnes to Cheshire, St Helens to Merseyside. ESRL decided to abandon the old County concept and to look instead to a future in two regions; East of the Pennines and West of the Pennines. It is perhaps sometimes overlooked that each

September every School or District must build a completely new side. As a voluntary body, every penny is spent directly on the game: no wages are paid, indeed hundreds of schoolmasters must be out of pocket every week because of their love for the game.

Editorial - England v France Programme, 1977

The Hull Association is not jumping on the post-Australian tour 'band wagon,' nor are we taking part in the 'knocking' of our national body, ESRL. In response to the Hon. Secretary's request to come to this meeting and explain 'many weaknesses' in the ESRL organisation, such a suggestion came after the Hull Officers had spent some two years deliberating on our own Association's future and one vital issue was always at the forefront of our thinking, the playing of rugby league and its growth and development was paramount. We called for total teacher support. You all know that this has not been forthcoming anywhere and the situation worsens season by season.

Today we can call upon almost 100 lay-helpers. Enthusiastic teachers in Junior High School, able to field teams across the age range, are being supported by parents and lay-helpers when help from their own colleagues is not forthcoming - and this with the Association's support and blessing! The schoolteacher remains in charge of organisation and administration. This season, both Leeds and Warrington U16 teams were controlled by lay-helpers. Presumably, Rule 5 of Competition Rules could have been applied and prevented these games taking place. There is no direct access to statistics but it would be interesting to see who currently organises the most schoolboy rugby league - ESRL or BARLA? Gentlemen, one of our basic objects is to promote and organise rugby league football for schoolboys. Are we fulfilling that role?

ESRL Divisional competitions have not been successful and that is said despite Hull's outstanding record. We have always been advocates of the scheme but have grown weary of the constant travel into SW Lancashire. We have even contemplated asking for affiliation to NW Counties. Despite the struggles to maintain Division 1 teams without Division 1 talent, we have to go back into the schools where it all begins, encouraging regular local games, then on to games over the Region. This will require a radical change in the financial arrangements between the Region and the Local Associations. You will, I am sure, hear more of this!
ESRL has a major part to play. There has to be links with all facets of the game, RFL, BARLA, BUSCARLA, Referees, Coaching Association, etc., meeting at least once a year to thrash out policies of communal interest, a continuous dialogue between the groups all the time, certainly at officer level and also in the form of written communications. We cannot remain in isolation.

The dramatic drop in teacher-interest in all extra-curricular activities, coupled with a halt in the steady flow of young men into the profession makes the problem urgent - five years will be too late!! If the game is to thrive, then our senior clubs have to accept their responsibilities towards finance, organisation and coaching at all school levels.

Discussion document presented to an ESRL Executive Meeting held at Huddersfield on Friday 18th February, 1983

There was a significant amount of schools rugby played in Hemel during the mid to late 90s - unearthing talent such as Jack Howieson and Simon Tillyer. The later 'boom' time was due in part to a hefty SE grant for 'active sports' which ironically wasn't supposed to fund school sport! I remember a particularly effective 2000 RLWC project which involved a good programme in Reading (run by James Massara) and

English Schools' Rugby League

First Test Match
Schoolboys

ENGLAND

v

AUSTRALIA

CENTRAL PARK, WIGAN
(BY KIND PERMISSION OF THE DIRECTORS)

SATURDAY, 30th DECEMBER, 1972
Kick-off 2-30 p.m.

Souvenir Programme 5p

---

also led to a wet but exciting tournament at Twickenham - and the kids got to meet the first reality TV band Hearsay. James did an amazing project with a group of girls from the Guru Nanak school, who played St Thomas More girls school from North London before the Australia v NZ game in 2005. Ashley Klein turned up for a North London schools tournament – the first time anyone had met this Aussie backpacker - with full NRL refs kit, two whistles and a heart-rate monitor.

Caro Wild, then RFL development officer London & South

The care and concern of teachers was pre-eminent. Many of the boys had great difficulty in obtaining the necessary gear to participate. As a consequence, the schools, through their schoolmasters, took on the task of obtaining the funds necessary to purchase jerseys, shorts and rugby boots where necessary.

Perhaps it would be appropriate to remind ourselves that most boys then wore clogs, and some even played matches in them. The teachers have also been assisted by many eminent men from outside the teaching profession, who have given financial and personal encouragement over the years. Pre-eminently, the Earl of Derby, and his son the present Lord Derby. We are proud to be able to claim their support since the foundation of this body. They have shed light and lustre and the present Lord Derby maintains a keen interest in our activities.

Lancashire County Schools Rugby League 1913–1988 - An Appreciation by F Howarth B.A. Past Chairman - Life Member

Travel was by coach, Messrs Danby's of Hull, with owner Ted Danby sharing driving with his assistant Brian. A long journey to Ramsgate was continued the following morning with a quick hovercraft crossing of a choppy Channel - and 455 miles later Limoges was reached for overnight stay. The following day Pamiers was the destination and the party were put up at the Les Parets school, in dormitory conditions. A magnificent reception afterwards introduced the party to such exotic fare as guinea fowl and all were glad to reach their billets. A game was fixed for the little village of Valderies, in hilly surroundings. The boys changed in a hut on the edge of the field; washing facilities consisted of baths outside the huts and other facilities such as toilets were also limited as two members of staff found out to their disadvantage as the game progressed.

One boy, late in arrival surveyed the crowded scene and craftily told some of the back substitutes 'Mr Jolley wants to see you'. On departing he promptly sat down in the vacated place before confiding in Mr Norris, 'and they think us prop forwards are thick, sir!' After the Test in Villeneuve sur Lot, the Town Hall reception was harder as there was no one to interpret and it was 11.30pm before the last boy was accommodated after a very tiring day and later still when the organisers including Messrs Profitt and Causey saw the rest off to bed, or nearly so - the snoring of a certain member of the party forcing Mr Causey to complete the tour by sleeping in a downstairs armchair.

France, 1974

Got those jerseys out. They were pre war. They were like goalie's - polo neck things and green and woolly. They were awful to be honest.

August, start of season, you got hot and everything started to itch. It was murder, you couldn't get your breath. They were soccer boots in them days - brown 'uns with big, hard toe caps. They weighed a ton with leather studs not metal. The ball was the old leather thing. Sometimes we couldn't get it to go ten yards - it was that heavy.

I was captain of the team when I got to be 13, 14 and they used to give me the bus fare for everybody. It was tuppence apiece. I'd ask the conductor 'fourteen tuppennies', he was rolling 'em off like a streamer. Worse was not being able to get a bath. We'd come back home plastered up sometimes during the winter. Nobody taught me the rules, I learnt 'em as we played.

John Sheridan, one of the most admired characters in the sport

Wembley was one of those moments you could never forget. We had raised sufficient money to make a weekend of it for the boys and the squad and coaches left on Friday morning, with a parents and supporters coach coming down the following day. The kids were treated like the professional finalists, with a visit to the hallowed turf and tour of the stadium on the Friday, followed by a trip around London and a museum before staying overnight at the Wembley Hilton.

That in itself was not without problems with a few of the boys fooling around and one player Dean Armitage falling down stairs and hurting his ankle. He had to be omitted from the team because he could hardly walk, but he begged us not to take him to hospital until after the match. He even did the run of honour across the pitch after the match with the two squads and received his medal before being taken to hospital in London that evening by his parent to discover he had a broken ankle.

I am not sure what the Child Protection people today would make of that, but his parents felt he should not miss the occasion despite the bad luck of not being able to play and I couldn't argue with that.

Ian Anniss, Sheffield Eagles Board member

We got invited to the Warrington All England 7s. Must have heard we'd got a good side.

All the best in the north of England played there. We got the invite very late on - the kids had just started the Easter holiday and the tournament was at the end.

I had to go round parents and say, 'Can you come up to

LANCASHIRE SCHOOLS' RUGBY LEAGUE

20 Crosfield Street,
WARRINGTON WA1 1UD

25th February, 1976

Dear Colleague,

The following boys have been selected to represent West of the Pennines v. East of the Pennines, to be played at Odsal Stadium, Bradford, on 6th March, 1976.

Under 13 (Kick off 1.30 p.m.)		Under 16 (Kick off 2.30 p.m.)	
Chaddefton	Oldham	Trainor	St.Helens
Hardman	Warrington	Bentley	Widnes
Shaw	Widnes	McTigue	Wigan
Davies	Leigh	France	Wigan
Stott	Oldham	Horne	Barrow
Clough	Wigan	Peters	St.Helens
Chesters	Barrow	Bucys	Leigh
Burke	Wigan	Sarsfield	St.Helens
Ruane	Widnes	O'Neill	Wigan
Lowndes	Warrington	Rabbitt	Leigh
Wood	Leigh	Peake	Wigan
Whitehead	Oldham	Stockley	Wigan
Lloyd	Leigh	Morgan	Wigan
Substitutes selected from:-		Substitutes selected from:-	
Morgan	Widnes	Dawson	Oldham
Crompton	Leigh	Ashurst	Wigan
Quinn	Leigh	Henney	Whitehaven
Leonard	St.Helens	Nee	St. Helens
Galloway	Wigan	Snee	Widnes
Referee: Mr. Knowles Leigh		Referee: Mr. McHugh Wigan	
Linesman: Mr.Watkinson Wigan		Linesman: Mr. Mallen Wigan	

All players must provide white shorts, properly studded boots and towel.

Travel Arrangements:

Coach will depart TOWN HALL, ST. HELENS, 9.40 a.m. and pick up at CARVER PLACE, SANKEY ST. WARRINGTON 10.00 a.m. BEAMONT SCHOOL, LONG LANE, WARRINGTON 10.10 a.m. x MANCHESTER ROAD SCHOOL, LEIGH 10.35 a.m. MILNROW ROUNDABOUT, M.62 11.05 A.M. and stop for refreshments at Hartshead Service Station M.62, departing there at 12.15 p.m. to arrive at Odsal Stadium at 12.30 p.m.

Secretaries are requested to inform all concerned.

Yours sincerely,
N.C. JOLLEY
Hon. Secretary

x Parking available

Distribution: President, Chairman, Vice Chairman, Hon.Treasurer, Hon. Secretaries of Associations mentioned above.

the High School and we'll train and go through some moves?' They listened attentively and asked questions for about an hour and a half. I was absolutely gobsmacked! I kept looking at the parents to say, 'Shall I get off now' and they kept giving me thumbs up, I kept going... and they won the tournament.

Roy Homer

Rugby league in secondary schools was very, very important in Castleford, it wove the whole social fabric of the area together. The schools, while being friendly, were very keenly competitive. There was an excellent co-operation between all the teachers and particularly the Head teachers, who realised that this was a way of character-building amongst the boys. I don't think it particularly fostered any macho image but the boys who were in the team were

A tradition is born - referee Stephen Bateson points to the spot as Widnes post a try against Wigan in the first-ever Wembley curtain-raiser for U11s in 1975

looked up to very much by the others, without any real jealousy. We were financed by Yorkshire Schools Rugby League, who got a grant from the Rugby Football League at the time, but also to a certain extent by Castleford. Teachers would man the boys' and girls' junior gates for free. Castleford would also issue free tickets to all schoolboy rugby league players in the area. The teachers would check them through because they would know the faces.

We would play any night of the week, Saturday mornings even Saturday afternoons. We never played Sundays for the impossibility that schools were shut and, as everybody knows, caretakers were the most important person on the premises. We had to keep them on our side. It worked incredibly well and there were very, very few occasions on which the fixture would fall down or players not turn up. Everything was done to make a fixture go ahead. We didn't live in the lap of luxury. The boys would walk a couple of miles there and even get changed on the touchline if there were no suitable changing rooms. Sometimes, you had touch judges. Sometimes the teacher just had to rely on the honesty of the boys. I cannot recall any occasions on which there were disputes. The spirit was really excellent.

Everybody wants to score, we were very successful in creating teams as well as gifted individuals. It was teaching them to blend together. That was the job that I saw I had to do. We had to train defensive structures as well - like corner flagging. They now call it scrambling defence. It was a very friendly atmosphere. In fact, it might sound a bit strange nowadays, you'd even have conversations between the ref and people on the touchlines as the scrums were forming.

Castleford Boys nearly won the Yorkshire Cup for the third time in a row. We were playing Belle Isle, Hunslet. Our second row took the ball and cut out to the wing and I was the touch judge. His boot just brushed the whitewash and I had to raise my flag. But, he was unaware. He carried on and went and scored under the posts, which would have been the winning try. The whole of the team jumped up in exhilaration. They thought they'd won the match. And they turned round, to see me, their own teacher, raising his flag. They didn't know whether to laugh, cry or murder me but it had to be done.

Michael Bates

I was probably the oldest player to take part in an U16 match, coming on for a combined McEntee/Daneford team against the touring Newland Y.C. from Hull. At that stage the visitors were ahead 15-1. The sight of a bearded adult coming on for the opposition may have caused comment amongst the Hull lads but hardly consternation for they carried on where they left off and ran out winners by 33 points to 1.

Mick Smyth, teacher at a girls' secondary school in Camberwell

The man behind schools rugby league development in the town says the programme will continue despite Government and RFL funding cuts. Neil Kelly is director of the Warrington Wolves Charitable Foundation which runs coaching programmes and development programmes across the town. The foundation is starting its bid to raise the £50,000 needed to keep the coaches in employment with a bucket collection ahead of the Warrington Wolves v Castleford Tigers match on Sunday. "We will get the money, there is no doubt about that. When fans come to the game, they see Chris Riley from Penketh High, Mike Cooper from Bridgewater, Tyrone McCarthy from Lysander."

Warrington Guardian, January 2013

Different Class

I attended a primary school housed in an imposing Victorian building on York Road – Victoria County Primary. Despite it being a soccer school there was a large and significant group of us who's first love was rugby league and who spent every spare minute playing various versions of the game. At school, because there wasn't a blade of grass in sight, this invariably meant a game of touch rugby played - on some occasions - with the luxury of a tennis ball, but more often than not with some other object found on the way to school that morning: a plastic lemon; an old shoe or glove; a tin can; but mostly, a stone lying in some corner of the playground that by the following day seemed to have mysteriously vanished.

In the secondary school environment not only was there the chance to play rugby league in our timetabled games lessons, but, joy of joys, there was after school rugby as well, with an opportunity to play in the school teams. This was the land of fantasy not only proper shirts, and a real ball but a team with which to identify.

Philip Haller

We got our own team together with the help of Arthur Kitson a really talented boy at the school. We were all mates and Mr Tarpey our PT instructor gave us his support. We played in all colours of shirts and socks scrounged from mates. We had a garden at school which produced the veg for us, we still had rationing. Rugby league was our social life.

Brian Nettleton

5

*

Awaydays

Last weekend the Swinton Boys travelled to the Metropolis to represent Lancashire against Yorkshire Boys. They left Swinton on Friday evening, many of them on their first visit to London, full of excitement.

At Euston station they were met by Mr J Steele, of the Streatham and Mitcham R.L. Club and a number of Supporters' Club officials of the new London club. The boys were given an official welcome before moving on to their hotel in Earl's Court. On the next morning all the boys journeyed together to the Stadium.

There were 4,000 present the majority of whom were schoolboys from London. After the match both teams were entertained to lunch and welcomed as rugby league ambassadors, the first elementary schoolboys to play that type of rugby in London. After lunch both teams and teachers were taken to Wembley to see the cup final after which the boys returned to the hotel for dinner. The evening was spent in sightseeing and the boys were amazed at the wealth of the Jubilee decorations.

On Sunday morning they visited many of the historic places in London, and at noon a happy band of Lancashire lads boarded the 'Lancastrian' for home. We are grateful to the London club for financing this trip.

'London Calling' – Daily Dispatch article, May 1935

We beat York to earn our place at Wembley it was only after that match that the full impact really hit us. We were going to Wembley, at 10 years old! Where every rugby player dreams of going and few ever do. We were all kitted out in blazers and grey trousers, really looking professional. After our visit to the TV studio and being filmed for '*Blue Peter*', it was time to go that great stadium. The feeling as we ran up the tunnel was one of complete numbness. I remember feeling very small and very, very excited.

Paul Carty, who played at full back in
Leeds Schools' first U11 Wembley side in 1976.

In the afternoon we visited Wembley and were told what we had to do the following afternoon. (With the two Scott's from Kirkstall it took a long time!). Everyone woke up bright and early which was a surprise after the fun and games of the night before. Everyone was very nervous as we were getting changed, but the talk in the dressing room was not about the match but about Mr Edmondson wearing a tie and shoes. This proved just how important the game was.

Andrew Edgell

'A unique opportunity for schoolboys to play at Wembley on cup final day is being kicked into touch by the English Schools Rugby League.' These were the sensational headlines in this week's *Rugby Leaguer*. The idea put forward by Huddersfield Rugby League Referees' Society, and which received tremendous support from the senior clubs was for a 'National Seven-a-side' at U16 level to be played next season, in which any school in the country could enter. After a series of qualifying rounds - the two leading sides would then automatically play at Wembley prior to the cup final as part of the pre-match entertainment. The basic principle behind

The ESRL party in France, 1980, Lee Crooks in the middle along with Mike Gregory, Mark Conway, Des Foy and Russell Smith.

the scheme was to stop the drift of senior schools (13-16) to rugby union and at the same time share rugby league's annual showpiece with the 'grass roots' of the game, the schoolboys. The plans were eventually drawn up after consultations with local prominent schoolteachers. After many negotiations Chapeltown Road said that Wembley was available and they would be prepared to meet the costs of taking the two teams. Mr Eddie Waring has expressed great enthusiasm for the plan, whilst the Southern Amateur Rugby League have stated it would be a tremendous boost for the

ENGLISH SCHOOLS RUGBY LEAGUE

ENGLAND V FRANCE

WHITEHAVEN 8.4.77

INCOME			EXPENDITURE		
Advertising	90	00	Reception	240	60
C.E.C. Grant	48	60	Printing		
C.E.C. Match Ball	14	50	Programme	138	60
Gate Receipts	142	60	Invitations	11	10
Programme Receipts	138	50	Board Room	13	01
Half Time Draw	43	30	Presentations	56	25
Donations			Ref & Linesmen	20	00
Workington Town RLSC	25	00	Gratuity	5	00
J.H. Martin	2	00	Programme Sellers	3	20
K. Burns	2	50			
			Balance to E.S.R.L	19	24
	£ 507	00		£ 507	00

game in the London area. The English Schools, after accepting the idea of the National Sevens, which they will run next season, have stated, believe it or not, 'They do not want to play at Wembley - they see no positive advantage from playing such a final on Cup Final day.' It's almost unbelievable that the nominators of the schoolboy game should come to such a decision that deprives their own pupils of every schoolboy's dream - 'A Wembley appearance,' whilst the loss from a propaganda point of such a game and the resultant TV coverage is incalculable.

From Fartown's Christmas Programme 26th December, 1972

Two local schoolboys have been picked for the British Upper

Schools and Colleges Amateur Rugby League Association tour of Australia this summer. Philip Morris, of Airedale High School, and Castleford High's Iain Cockerham came out tops after the final trials at Knottingley High School. Philip, who is a professional with Oldham, was the first player to represent the county at schoolboy rugby league and union level. He is in the Upper Sixth at Airedale studying for his 'A' levels.

'Going down under' – article February, 1984

Two rugby league development areas met in a game at Crystal Palace when 36 Blackpool schoolboys between the ages of 9 and 15 came down for a week of sporting activities, under the guidance of Tom Mather and Graham Starkey and played Peckham Manor School at U14s level in an entertaining, close-run game.

Local newspaper report, 1979

Whilst I have such happy memories of my tour to France in 1976 unfortunately I do not have any photographs, programmes or the like to look back on. Regretfully this is the sort of thing you do not think about at 16 when enjoying yourself so much.

We were based in Lezignan and were made most welcome by the locals at civic receptions etc. My love of France continues as we holiday there each year. My centre was Keith Bentley from Widnes and we were very close buddies throughout the tour. Keith was a magic player at that age, he signed professional for Widnes when they were a top side and later in his career played some games for Barrow. Our bus driver played his Glen Campbell's Greatest Hits tape constantly for the whole tour.

John Horne from Golborne, who played for England schools on the third tour of France

This is a family occasion... Ever since 1933, a joint committee of the Leeds and Hunslet Schools' Rugby Leagues has organised a trip to London to enable the rugby-playing boys of the city to see the places of interest and then watch the Rugby League Cup Final at Wembley Stadium. On each post-war visit (since 1950), we have enjoyed our visit to the Tower of London, and then proceeded to Wembley Stadium with an almost detached interest in the game and the result. Not so this year. Things are vastly different: LEEDS is one of the finalists.

One still recalls the bubbling anticipations of 1934 and 1936, when first Hunslet and then Leeds went to triumph at Wembley ... the thrill when Jim Brough, the Leeds captain, standing on the apron (where is it now?) proudly 'showed' the Cup to our cheering party. Our satisfaction was heightened because 'Yarry' Isaac, loose forward in the 1936 Leeds team, was a teacher in Leeds. This Leeds team, managed by Ken Dalby, a former official of the Leeds Schools' Rugby League, has strong local associations. The captain, Keith McLellan, and Pat Quinn (full-back) are teachers well known at Middleton and Harehills, while five of the team played in local schools' rugby. This long day out is organised in great detail and it is most important that you should follow the instructions so that nothing comes unstuck. Bring your overcoat (or raincoat and something warm under it), for you will be in the open at Wembley.

See that your badge label is filled in and tie it to your jacket. (Hide it in your breast pocket if you wish, but it must be TIED TO YOU - and you won't get on the platform unless it is). Pack some sandwiches (to eat at Wembley before the match begins). You might like to bring a few sweets (for there will be little chance to buy any during the day), but choose pastilles, gums, boiled sweets and nothing that is sticky, sickly or likely to melt in your pocket.

IAN BRIDGE

Ian Bridge is from Mannering Park and attends Wyong High School. Ian who weighs 9 stone 10 pounds plays half-back and has represented his district since he was 8 years old. He also captained Sydney Metropolita N9 stone team and is keen on cricket, swimming and sailing.

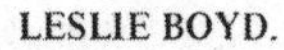

LESLIE BOYD.

Hails from Nyngan is a hard running forward who has represented his school at swimming, cricket and atheletics. Leslie is 5 feet 8 inches and weighs 12stone 7 pound.

TREVOR BINSKIN.

Trevor Binskin, of Kariong, attends Gosford High School. He weighs 10 stone 5 pound is 5 feet 9 inches and his position is hooker. Trevor has represented Central Coast and played for N.S.W. against New Guinea 9 stone 1971. He is a keen surfer.

Taken from the tour brochure produced by the inaugural Australian Schoolboy tourists in 1972 and containing a soon-to-be familiar name

Bring a piece of pencil or a ball-point pen (for the essay competition on the way back). Bring some pocket money (for minerals etc.) Stick to the teacher in charge of you: Never let him out of your sight.

On the train, the coaches are lettered 'A' to 'M' (but there is no 'I'). You must not wander from coach to coach - discipline will be strict about this - and you must not remain in the end sections of the coaches. Don't fiddle with the windows or doors. You don't have to be told how dangerous this is - and (owing to railway regulations) certain doors cannot be locked which means you must be even more careful. A packed meal and a mineral will be brought to you on the train (and also on the return journey). Don't drink the water in the toilet washbasins. There will be prizes for the tidiest carriages. If you get lost, anywhere on the trip, show your badge label and this handbook to a policeman and ask him if he can see that you get to King's Cross Station before 6.45pm.

Leeds and Hunslet Schools'
Annual Trip to London and Wembley; May 11th, 1957

A representative eleven selected by the Widnes Schools's League, journeyed to Barrow on Saturday, to meet the Barrow Schoolboys' team. Widnes kicked off against a strong wind. Barrow pressed strongly, Fallowfield scoring at the corner. Barrow continued the pressure, long kicks spoiling their efforts. Later Hocknell scored. Hosker saved grandly time after time. Lipear played brilliantly, but the backs could not make headway. From a mark in front of goal an unsuccessful attempt to add points was made. With the aid of the wind, it was expected that the Widnes team would make havoc of the home team, but this was not so.

Inter-School League -7th April, 1909

It must have seemed a giant step to the officers of the newly formed English Schools R.L. when they accepted the invitation of M Paul Tancrede of Carcassonne to bring a party of schoolboys to the area for the purpose of initiating competition at that level. The visit was arranged to coincide with the All Saints national holiday in 1967. The journey was by rail-boat-rail. The sea was so rough that mal de mer soon set in and made the crossing thoroughly unpleasant. Yet undaunted everybody had recovered on arrival, the party being based in the Auberge de Jeunes in the old Cite. During the day the boys were hosted out to French families but all returned to the Youth Hostel by 22.00 hours.

29 Oct (Sun) v Carcassonne XIII won easily 31-3. Reception followed presided over by M Tancrede and M Forges (French RL), officials of the local clubs A.S.C. and St Jacques and representatives from Villeneuve and Perpignan.

1 Nov (All Saints) v Languedoc XIII at the St Jacques club gave the second team opportunity to play and they won narrowly 8-5.

2 Nov - a long journey to St Gaudens to play a Comminges side at the invitation of the brothers who ran the local club, and also successfully ran the pubic abbatoir! - won 28-2.

3 Nov - Free day and a visit to the 'Caves' at Limoux, the local wine cellars, not a trip down a pothole. Following day via the Pyrenees to the Font Romeu Olympic training centre and on to Perpignan for overnight stay.

5 Nov. - Customary reception at the Perpignan club - first ever schoolboy Test game took place as curtain raiser to a local senior club game. The final score of 17-2 to the visitors did not indicate the closeness of the contest. As the club game was without a referee, Mr Gibson was soon pressed into service and created quite an impression when after a fracas he sent both teams off the field to cool down with the comment, 'I'm not allowing stuff like this.'

ESRL prepare to face France at Craven Park, Hull in 1979. Back row (left to right) Walter Norris (coah), Allan Platt, Robert Kettle, Ian Sheldon, Jeffrey Brown, Steven Walsh, Ian Hall, Lee Crooks, Paul Lowndes, Barney O'Hara (manager) Front row (left to right) Stuart Wardle, Des Foy, Gary Standkins, Chris Willis, Shaun Patrick, David Hewitt, Paul Chester, Francis Clough.

Facilities provided had been excellent, hospitality out of this world but the rail-sea marathon very tiring to say the least. Total cost had been £900; boys had contributed £5 each and the remainder met by grants from local associations, County RL bodies, the Rugby Football League and the DES. It was hoped to return the compliment in 1968 but the parlous state of ESRL finances following the visit precluded an invitation.

Barney O'Hara – described by his peers as 'a tough Irishman who never held back' and who went on to become Chairman of the ESRL, describing the first tour to France in 1967

We had a training session where an *Evening Post* photographer and reporter were there to take a team photo and that's when it sunk in. The headline read 'Wembley Boys Are Doing Fine' and I really felt we were going. My grandparents live on the Isle of Man and as soon as they knew, the flights were booked, in fact I was headline news in one of the local papers! There was a full page about me, my hobbies, rugby and my mum and dad.

One abiding memory of the build up to Wembley was going to the house where the parents of the legendary Leeds winger John Atkinson lived, he came round and told me about playing at Wembley and how nervous he had been. We set off on the Friday morning, we were booked into the very luxurious Wembley Conference Hotel. An evening meal was followed by a visit to the *Guinness Book of Records* Exhibition, and then an early night - did we really keep Ray French and Alex Murphy up all night? After breakfast on the big day we were called into the coach's room to find out the actual team; this was the moment some of us had been dreading. There were 18 of us in the squad, of which only 15 could play; we all sat on two beds looking at each other and knowing that there would be some upset lads. We looked at the three lads who were not picked, they had tears in their eyes.

Dean Buckler

As a boy growing up in Sheffield I'd never having heard of rugby league but had always been sport mad. When playing days were over a good friend encouraged me to take up rugby league refereeing. In the back of my mind was still the dream of Wembley. Imagine my excitement when I received a letter last November inviting me to referee the schoolboy curtain-raiser. Friday 1st May I set off: I had to be at the ground for 1pm to meet the teams, rehearse coming onto the pitch and what happens after the game, and then went to our plush hotel, and finally went to bed to find I could not sleep. The big day came and when I arrived at the ground the only people who seemed to be nervous were the two touch judges and me. I remember the thrill of walking out onto the pitch and my legs feeling like lead. Very soon we were back in the changing room and all the boys signed the match ball. I wonder how many of them will become big stars in the future.

Peter Woodhead

The British Aerospace Junior Lions' Queensland tour is the culmination of many years of commitment and dedicated preparation. The recent introduction of the U16 Premiership has moved the game forward both in the quality of competition and in national expansion. Teams from London, South Wales, Hemel Hempstead, St Albans, the North-East, Scarborough and Cleveland have joined. How exciting it is to see a London boy achieving selection for the national squad! More are expected as ESRL continues its expansion plans: Brighton have taken to the game with enthusiasm, there are promising developments in Ireland

"Right! You've had five minutes — now it's our turn."

● 1985 cartoon from the *'Wakefield Express'* after their schoolboys triumph at Wembley.

---

and in fact Dublin Schools' U11s played in this year's Wembley curtain-raiser and, hopefully, the pioneering work being done in Scotland may soon bear fruit. We are delighted that NASUWT, the career teachers' organisation, who are in the middle of a three year sponsorship which has been a massive aid in providing rugby league to the nation's boys and girls.

Peter Dawson, former Chairman ESRL

I look back over my involvement with fond memories. Training weekends in Oldham; is there a colder place on God's earth than Oldham in March? Parkfield Hotel, where Bobbie Goulding informed me, (some years later I might add), that he had sneaked in through a window late one

Roy Dickinson and Neil Hague dish out the prizes in 1985 including to a young James Lowes, (kneeling, fifth from left)

night whilst Barney O'Hara, the Team Manager, and I had been waiting in the foyer to discipline late comers. Having an Irish passport caused Barney a few problems coming back in to the country. I well remember him kneeling on the floor at Manchester airport with the contents of his suitcase scattered around him as, with much cursing, he informed all and sundry that he must have packed his passport. In 1984 we also had a budding entrepreneur with us in the shape of Tony Rowbottom. Tony took large supplies of paracetamol to France and sold them to the other lads at 10 francs per tablet. Two years later we were billeted in a small village with nothing for the lads to do in the evenings so I decided to organise a 'concert'. Former chairman, Fred Howarth started the ball rolling by playing a tune on the spoons. Barney and I did a 'magic' act and then it was the lads' turn. We had a Humberside prop named Lance Cator who was as broad as he was tall. A group of the players entered the room, surrounding Lance, who was wearing a dressing gown. They separated to leave Lance to do his act and he proceeded to peel off the dressing gown to reveal that he was wearing a full red negligee that he had bought for his girlfriend! To the tune of 'Hi Zigazumba', he then did a full Monty. I am sure that this did more for team bonding than anything I said all week.

In 1988 it was the turn of Graham Southernwood to provide the notable incident. We won the Test match and were given a superb reception at St Laurent, where the wine flowed freely. Early morning before the flight home, Graham was in no fit state to travel anywhere. We literally dragged him through Customs expecting to hear, 'Step this way sir' at any moment. Every tour has its notable moments. One year, I remember packing a case of red wine in the kit bags, only to find six of the twelve bottles smashed on retrieval at baggage collection. The short journey through Customs has never seemed so long and I still don't know how they missed the trail of red wine that I left behind. The white England kit was also in a sorry state. One year the squad won by 50 points to 2, despite a penalty count of 20 to 1 against us.

Touring memories - Dennis McHugh

'Thank goodness that's over.' No pupils lost, no pupils gained, no irate letters from hosts to the head! And yet, despite whatever relief there might be, we schoolmasters continue to organise them and enjoy them. I well remember my early days in touring with my own school, Cowley, and pacing up and down the coach as we journeyed up the M1 on our return from London. 'How many lads did we actually bring then? Why didn't you tell me he had gone to the toilet at the service station after I had counted you all?' Yes, the joys and tribulations of leaving a player behind at the Motorway Service Station. Suddenly peace is restored when a hooter sounds in the outside lane and grubby face peers up at the coach, banging frantically at the window of a Porsche. Your lost soul has proved the ingenuity of rugby players and hitched a lift. The joys of touring!

Ray French, dual international, teacher and BBC broadcaster

I can always remember the day I was selected for England. I couldn't wait to get home. My dad was a lorry driver so he was away. I felt really proud. I went in and said 'Mam! I've been picked to play for England.' She said, 'Where?' and I said, ' In France!' She said, 'We'll have to buy you a new suit or a new coat and trousers.' We all met at Leeds station. Mum came with me which is a bit iffy - I'm a fourteen year old lad. Five foot ten. It was the first time I'd been on a ferry. We'd never been abroad before. It was a foul day - force eight - quite a lot of the lads were sick. We got the train from

there to Paris, were based at Carcassone. A smashing place to a lad, it's got the best preserved medieval castle in Europe. To save money, they billeted us out with French families. I was taken two or three miles outside the city to it looked like a market garden farm. The lady in charge, she was the archetypal French woman farmer - massive! She kept giving me food, some sort of potato omelette. The only thing I wasn't too happy about was that we weren't given anything

The motif on the back of the 1988 programme as the French Cadets prepare to take on the ESRL side in Roussillon.

---

to commemorate being on the first English Schools tour. They didn't give us a shirt which I would have really loved, a badge, a medal, anything.

Keith Worsley, 1967 tour

7 - 13 July - In Brisbane
10 July - v Brisbane Independent Schools
13 July - Travel to Toowoomba (approx 1 1/2 hours) v Toowoomba Select
13-16 July - In Toowoomba
16 July - Travel to Kingaroy (approx 2 1/2 hours) v Wide Bay (Kingaroy)
16-18 July - In Kingaroy
18 July - Travel to Rockhampton (approx 5 hours)
19 July - v Rockhampton
18-21 July - In Rockhampton
21 July - Travel to Bundaberg (approx 4 hours)
22 July - v Bundaberg

21-23 July - In Bundaberg
23 July - Travel to Brisbane (approx 4 hours)
25 July - v Brisbane Representative Team (Redcliffe RLFC)
26 July - Depart

Junior Lions' Queensland Tour, July 1999 - Itinerary

Through the efforts of Mr Lee the possibility of air travel had been looked into at an early stage and thanks to the efforts of WGT Travel a flight from Heathrow to Bordeaux had been arranged. Only problem turned out to be films spoiled in luggage by the metal detector at the airport! A free day to the Pyrenees and town of Esperaza, a very interesting visit was made to a factory producing all kinds of pennants, stickers etc. and thanks to the kindness of the Blanquette de Limoux firm, all the party were presented with T-shirts printed while-

Hull K.R. and New Zealand captain Gordon Smith congratulates the captains of Bransholme High U14s, U15s and U16s who all won their Yorkshire Cups under the proud stewardship of Ged Dunn.

Copy of letter sent to Frank Hughes & [illegible] Barrows.

ENGLISH SCHOOLS' RUGBY LEAGUE

Tel: School (0942) 726842
Home (0695) 624104

20, Greenways,
Billinge,
Wigan,
Lancs.
WN5 7DF

February, 1984

Dear

Congratulations, you have been selected for the England U16s Squad to tour France at Easter, 1984. The Squad will leave Heathrow on Friday, 13th April at 19.50 hours on Flight No. AF 1823 and will return from Toulouse on Monday, 23rd April on Flight No. AF 1822 arriving at Heathrow at 9.40 a.m. During the tour matches will be played at Toulouse, Carcassonne and Arignon, culminating in a Test Match at Le Pontet.

Twenty-four boys have been selected and each boy will be expected to contribute £80 towards the cost of the Tour. (Show this letter to your teachers and other interested bodies since this money can usually be raised in your own district). You will also need pocket money, a passport, training gear, two pairs of white shorts, two pairs of white socks and a pair of white laces.

In preparation for the Tour the Squad will assemble at Parkfield Country Club, Oldham as follows:-

11.30 a.m. Friday 23rd March until after lunch on Sunday 25th March.

11.30 a.m. Friday 6th April until after lunch on Sunday 8th April.

Transport for boys from Yorkshire and Humberside will be arranged by Mr. B. O'Hara - Tel: (0484) 656584. I will arrange transport for boys from North West Counties.

For both these meetings you will need at least two sets of training gear including boots and training shoes. You will be staying for two nights in a top class hotel with swimming pool, sauna and squash courts so please wear clothing suitable for the occasion. In addition, to the first session, you should bring your £80 contribution, your passport and, if possible, your pocket money for changing into francs and safe-keeping by Mr. J. Lee, the Treasurer.

If you have any queries please do not hesitate to contact me on the numbers shown.

Yours sincerely,

D. McHugh

Coach - ESRL

you-wait 'TOURNEE CADETS MARS 1978'. Following a tasting session of Blanquette (by the adults) a marvellous four course repast ensued lasting a mere two hours!

France trip 1978

At Whitwood Mere, the Headmaster was totally supportive, Mr Crossley. I could have taken a team off all day because he knew it was doing them good. There were no fixture lists. It was all on and ad hoc basis so it meant breaking off from full time teaching to make a phone call in the cook's area. We travelled by service bus or I did use the car occasionally. I made three journeys once or twice. I had to somehow organise it so staff could take them and then high tail it back to school to take their own lessons. On the service bus kids paid their own fare.

Roy Homer

I was invited several times by the French League to go over to Limoges. I can remember going to Wallace Arnold. I spoke to the manager - 'I want to take two teams to the South of France.' He got back to me and said, 'it would cost you forty odd pounds per person'. £25 in those days was probably two weeks' wages.

Michael Bates

Wembley - to see 18 kids when they won it in front of 90,000 at 11 or 12 years of age; it is a one-off lifetime experience. When that final whistle went and everyone was crying and we all ran on the pitch and jumped on each other. When the kids talk about it, they'll cry. It was so emotional and that will stick with them for the rest of their lives.

Lee Hudson, teacher

It was a bright Sunday in April,
We were on our way,
Over the tops by bus
To Warrington to play.
I looked straight across the aisle,
And saw the great J.T.
Talking tactics there with Roy
Almost sitting on his knee.
Getting changed, rubbing legs

Different Class

The smell of embrocation
Only one thing needed now
The pitch and its location.
Final whistle sounded grand
Now it was all over
We'd won the shield and trophies too
Everyone in clover.

The Sage Of '74 - All England Sevens, by P.J. Hirst

Wembley to play in curtain raisers for the U11s were fantastic weekends. We stayed at the Wembley Hilton and then probably the best bit was when we went to see a West End show - *Starlight Express*.

Keith Banks

One of the great experiences of Leeds Schools Rugby League was the annual trip to Wembley for the Rugby League Challenge Cup final. My first experience was in my first year at Cross Green Comprehensive in 1965 when Hunslet played Wigan. The trip departed early on the Saturday morning when every school in Leeds met at city station to board a specially chartered train to New Southgate station in North London. How they managed to organise it I'll never know as the whole concourse was jam-packed with schoolchildren.

It was lively on the train going down and there seemed to be an absence of teachers, although they appeared miraculously at any hint of misdoing – such as leaving your seat. The arrival in London consisted of an orderly disembarkation from the train, past confused looking

Winners at Wembley in 1981, Castleford's schoolboy stars salute the packed crowd

uniformed British Rail personnel onto specially chartered coaches which would take us on a tour of London then disgorge us on the embankment to give us an hour or so to look round. The whole of the city seemed to be full of Leeds schoolchildren sporting chocolate and white rosettes.

The journey back reminded us all that we were on a school trip, as once on the train our teachers appeared with reams of paper and pencils. Surely they weren't going to do the unthinkable and ask us to write about our experiences. We looked at each other and gulped. "Do we have to?" "Yes you do" They smiled. How wise they were, for peace descended for an hour as we struck various angles of repose and recounted our experiences of the day. As the papers were collected, the effort of it all caught up with us and we crashed into a stupor of deep exhaustion.

Philip Haller

I shared a room with Mick Foster who went to Batley Parish School. When we were getting ready for bed I noticed Mick had a glass of water on his table. Suddenly he took his eye out and put it in the glass. I never realised he had a glass eye until then.

We were all supposed to wear the same type of boots which were from a sponsor. Mine were really uncomfortable so I wore a pair of my own. I can remember in the game one of the boots came off and I spent three or four minutes trying to get it back on. After the game some of the lads were buying beer from a kiosk. They were caught and we all got lined up and were given a dressing down. Mick and me were probably the only ones that weren't involved but we still got told off.

Francis Maloney, played professionally with distinction for 19 years, however, it was as a nine-year-old that he made his only Wembley appearance in the 1983 curtain raiser.

6

*

The Unsung

I first played rugby league at the age of 12 when I went to Rawthorpe Secondary School. The first person to get me involved was our sports teacher Brian Skerry. He saw me play my first ever game in the games lesson and asked me if I would bring my kit the day after and play for the second year team as we did not have a team in the first year.

Brian Blacker, ex-Huddersfield

One of the great characters was undoubtedly Jack McGuire who was chairman of Wigan and Lancashire Schools RL in the 1920s and 30s. His differences of opinion with a Mr Ashburner of St Helens were legendary and became so rancorous that both were ousted from Lancashire Schools. Jack begun his teaching career at St Patrick's Wigan and under his tutorship the school became the inaugural winner of the *Daily Dispatch* Shield in 1926 before a crowd of 16,000 at Central Park. He moved to St Joseph's. In 1936-37 and 1937-38 the school won the *Daily Dispatch* Shield, the first to win it in successive seasons.

Jimmy Kearns was a member of the St Patrick's side in 1926. In one game Jack shouted from the touchline that the ball should be 'moved along the line'. Kearns had possession at that moment and heard the instruction but, being a quick witted lad, spotted half an opening, and with quick dummy

Dewsbury & Batley Schools Association pick their U11s squad for Wembley, 1983 Back row (left to right) D. Ward (asst coach), E. Wilby (asst coach), M. Foster, D. Comiskey, S. Ellam, J. Brookes, A. Holmes, S. Vickers, P. Goodall. P. Ganley (asst coach), P. Metcalfe (coach) Middle row (left to right) J. Dyson, D. Goodall, A. Holmes, A. Lay, I. Turton, N. Muston, J. Brierley, A. Shaw Front row (left to right) S. Wells, R. Stephenson, C. Lees, P Hinchliffe (capt), L. Lyman, F. Maloney, L. Wells.

ran through the opposition and scored a try to the delight of his team mates and of course himself. When the half time talk came along, Kearns, expecting a word of congratulation from his coach, developed a headache due to McGuire clouting him several times, whilst repeating over and over again, 'When I tell you to pass the ball, you pass the ball.'

Owd Jack and Young Jimmy

Mick Fieldhouse was recorded in 1965 trying to revive the game in schools, as was Albert Fearnley from Bradford Northern along with Trevor Foster. In 1995 Bradford Schools made their first appearance at Wembley, managed by Dave Jones and coached by Steve Fairhurst, John Simpson also assisted, Gary Tasker who was the Bradford Northern general manager and a former Bradford Schoolboy, worked tirelessly to revive RL in Bradford Schools, refereeing many matches in that time.

Bradford Schools Year Book

My first recollection of Walter 'Knocker' Norris was as an eleven year old in the late 1950s. Walter was my engineering workshop and sometimes technical drawing teacher at Beamont Secondary Technical School. Walter had recently qualified as a teacher having spent his formative years in industry - Richmond Gas Stores in Latchford, Warrington - serving his time as a tinsmith as well as playing part-time professional rugby league for Warrington and St Helens. As usual, there were the class comedians who tried their luck but nobody took Walter on twice. Although a hard task master he was always fair.

The rugby league ethos was endemic in the school such that teams were organised in the school yard to play 'tick and pass' at break times, lunch times and after school at 4.00pm. A rubber handle bar grip from a bicycle doubled up

as the ball. These bounced quite well off the tarmac surface and made for interesting kick offs. Consequently, many pupils rode around on bikes with no handle bar grips after their disappearance at an alarming rate from the bikes

The schoolboys of Hull and Widnes prepare to leave the Wembley stage

stored in the sheds in the school yard. Although Walter was not our official games master, he sometimes took charge of lessons when others were off ill or not available. Beamont Tech had no playing fields and rugby was played on the

Technical College field at Long Lane - a mile or so from the school in O'Leary Street. One vivid memory I have from the early 60s was of a cold winter day with a fierce wind and horizontal rain interspersed with violent showers of hailstone. With the wind chill factor, the temperature felt like minus five. The college playing fields at their best were a bog with all sides open to the elements. This was the era of unlimited tackles and it became a forward and scrum dominated game. Just before the end there was a break down the centre of the field and it became obvious the opposing full back had disappeared. There was a shrill blast of the whistle followed by 'Knocker's' bellowing voice. 'Where's Williams?' 'Gone for a shower Sir, he was cold!' 'COLD! - right you lot stay here.' Walter marched off the field to the changing rooms and returned five minutes later with Williams in tow saying, 'Get back on the field you big Nelly and play rugby. Never mind the cold, that won't harm you, but I might.'

Tony Hawley

Austin Kiernan became a County Selector in 1970 and was to serve in this capacity until 1993. A very astute character who saw potential in boys who would later become professionals, he travelled Yorkshire and Lancashire alongside Bernard O'Hara and Colin Murray. They became known as the 'Three Musketeers'. Bernard was a tough Irishman and he never held back when expressing his feelings. Eddie Shaw was a stalwart especially in the 90s when schools rugby was suffering badly from lack of staffing and the loss of Leagues. He tried his best to keep things going by concentrating on mini-tournaments and stopped the complete demise of schools rugby in the town at that time.

Huddersfield Schools minutes

I began my rugby league career at St Jude's school under the tutelage of Michael Mullaney. His charm, charisma and love of the game made it so attractive for me to get involved. Yes the Town's glittering history at professional level is largely responsible for that reputation but nobody should underestimate the role that Wigan Schools' RL has played.

Kris Radlinski, Wigan great

'Mac' as he was commonly known began teaching at St Patrick's School in 1947. He had a great memory and could recall each and every one of the players he coached, and would often reminisce with affection for them, whether at the bar in The White Horse, The Griffin or later at The Brocket whilst chain smoking to his heart's content.

Mac prided himself on his refereeing and he cut quite a dash in his trade-mark long shorts, which often caused hilarity. Anyone who saw him leading St Patrick's in the Whit Monday walks dressed in his top hat and tails, and greeting all and sundry who recognised him on the perambulations around the parishes, would have little doubt that he enjoyed and relished the 'oxygen of publicity'. Mac often employed a colourful turn of phrase though never involving a swear word.

Towards the end of his teaching career one season he took over the Wigan U11s Town Team. In his half time talk to the team during a game at Widnes, he told one player, who later became a professional, 'If you pass the ball one more time, I'll bring you off.'

He once told a BBC interviewer that all the training for rugby was done in St Patrick's School Yard, and that sometimes the boys' toilets overflowed which was useful because it showed which players were backs and which were forwards. The backs he said would sidestep the 'pee',

A West Yorkshire Police officer spends a lot of his spare time harassing Leeds headmasters.

Peter Deakin's aim is to persuade as many of them as possible to allow their pupils to play Rugby League.

Deakin is development officer for the British Upper Schools and Colleges Amateur Rugby League Association, which was formed just over a year ago in a bid to bridge the gap between under-16 Rugby and the universities and colleges.

The new organisation stage their first representative match on Saturday when the Yorkshire under-19s take on their Lancashire counterparts at Wigan's Central Park ground.

In the longer term, plans are in hand for a British party of 28 to tour Australia in July and August of next year to take on the renowned Australian Combined High Schools in two Tests.

Deakin's job right now, however, is to enter traditional Rugby Union strongholds in the Leeds area and try to tell the teachers what they are missing.

"It's a mammoth task," he admits. "Of 42 entries for our knock-out competition this year, Parkside High are the only Leeds representatives and the number of city schools playing R.L. at this 16 to 19 age-group can only be described as pathetic.

"We aren't trying to take over from Rugby Union in any way.

"The fact is that many of the pupils at these schools and colleges already play R.L. for other teams at weekends, so why not let them represent their school at the game?

"It's my job to persuade the headmasters and P.E. teachers that they would be fulfilling a need by letting the lads play R.L. and, from our association's point of view, this is a vital age-group for the development of the code."

The Roses match at Vigan will be a trial for election for the five-veek tour, which will ake in Western Austra-ia, Northern Territory, ueensland and New outh Wales.

MOVE TO BOOST RL IN SCHOOLS

By ROBERT MILLS

Fenton, whose older brothers play for Castleford's senior side, and Alan Hardisty's son Ian.

Yorkshire's squad (back row, from the left):

Ron England (assistant coach, Knottingley), Martin Crick (coach, St John Fisher), Jonathan Prescott (Huddersfield), Jonathan Walker (Wheelwright), John Ineson (St. John Fisher), Andrew Burgess (Airedale High), Chris Burdon (Knottingley), Iain Cockerham (Castleford High), Billy Marchant (Castleford High), Ian Hardisty (Castleford High), Robert Nobles (Greenhead, Huddersfield), Robert Jennings (Wheelwright), Steve Alderson (manager). Front row (from the left): Patrick Wilson (St. John Fisher), Philip Morris (Airedale), Matthew Oldroyd (St. John Fisher), Simon Cartwright (Knottingley), Wayne Fenton (Castleford), Richard Waite (Knottingley), Andrew Bender (St. John Fisher), Steve Potts (Castleford) and Andrew Hartley (Castleford).

The first BUSCARLA Yorkshire side, championed by Peter Deakin whilst the forwards would run through it. He had an eccentricity full of warmth, wit and, sometimes pedantry.

An appreciation of John McDermott – Coalopolis to Pie Eaters

What I will never forget is the support from the local Barrow Schools Association especially Arthur Spencer and Des Slavin.

Des ran the Barrow Boys side and struggled at times to raise a full team. Although not a teacher at my technical school, Des regularly took me to Wigan and the like for Lancashire trials and games all in the evenings and in his own time. His commitment was unbelievable. Arthur was involved with the English Schools Association and my head teacher at the time.

I will never forget him saying to me I have some good and bad news for you. The good is you have been selected to go on tour with England Schoolboys to France. The bad is you are sitting an 'O' Level Chemistry exam on the day the tour departs and your educations comes first.

Little did I know that Arthur was already putting in place a plan whereby I sat the exam on my own the day before and he kept me in complete isolation, staying at his home overnight and then personally getting me to a departure point in south Lancashire the next day.

John Horne

It all started for me with a casual chat with Fred Howarth after I had played for Oldham at Watersheddings. Fred, a former Headmaster in the town, was a real character. By then he was well into his 70s and still with an eye for the ladies.

Fred was good company and always fun to be with. His passion was rugby league; a founder member of English Schools and a true believer in the importance of the grass roots. After chatting up my lovely wife Anne for half an hour he then turned to me and asked why my school was not playing rugby league.

Phil Larder

I represented England schools at scrum half. I felt I arrived that day as a boy and left as a man.

Peter Chester

I have been living in Australia but grew up in Barrow-in-Furness. I attended Barrow Technical School from 1966 to 1968 and then moved to Walney Modern as it was known then. I played for the Barrow U13s as full back. It was a particularly good side. We were the first Barrow team to reach a Lancashire Cup final, beaten at Craven Park by Wigan. I still have the runners up medal. One of the reasons we did so well was because we had a stand off called Phil Hogan. I caught up with him a few years later when he was touring over here with Great Britain.

Some of the teachers involved were Mr Redhead, Mr Spencer and Mr Lancaster. In my first year at Tech I played in the team that won a local knockout competition. Billy Strickland virtually won it on his own. I think he also held an English Schools sprint title. A few years ago I was introduced to a bloke in a pub in Bomaderry (NSW South Coast) who was over from the UK on holiday. He said he was from Barrow and when we got talking it turned out we had both played against Wigan in that cup final. Obviously neither of us were tremendous players because we couldn't remember each other.

John Gallagher

On my way home to Jack Lane one evening after playing rugby on the moor, I called in at Aunt Lizzie's to show her

Hull schools take up a pioneering invitation to run coaching and administration seminars and play against Moscow Schools.

---

the new ball. Lizzie had known of my project, having given me jobs to provide the money. Never easily persuaded into conversations of any length, after hearing of my interest in rugby, she said: 'Ave you asked your uncle Bob about rugby?

The reformation of Hunslet was supported by the area's U11s who also wore the famous myrtle and flame colours.

He played with the Carr team ... They won all sorts of cups and medals.' Bob, expected to be on the threshold of a rugby or soccer career after leaving school, developed muscular rheumatism with complications. His heart was affected and doctors advised that future participation in active sport would be impossible. However, with my interest aroused, members of the family told me more about the teams, the players and their achievements. Bob played in both rugby and soccer teams, collecting some thirteen or fourteen medals. It has since been said by many that Mr Cripps at school level was the finest soccer and rugby coach ever. As the school's soccer coach at the time of Leeds City's fall-out with the F.A., due to his connection with the club he was barred from managing the soccer team. Undaunted, he formed a rugby side and the lads played soccer in the morning and rugby in the afternoon.

The lads trained daily, taking part in cross-country runs and other forms of exercise to keep them in peak of condition. Running back towards Hunslet Carr down the Old Run Road, from the fields of Belle Isle and Middleton, they stopped for a few minutes at a cottage near Hunslet Lane (the home of one of the boys) for cups of steaming-hot Oxo before returning to school and the resumption of lessons. In the evenings, particularly Friday evenings, Mr Cripps made spot checks on the homes of pupils to see if those picked to play on Saturday were in bed.

'Reflections of a Yorkie' - E A Lundy

The publication of this Handbook gives us our first opportunity of recording, publicly, the Yorkshire Schools' Rugby League's sincere appreciation of Mr Cripps' unselfish work on behalf of the schoolboys of Yorkshire. Over a long period of years Mr Cripps held the position of Secretary Organiser of the league, and it is largely due to his inspired and unstinted efforts that the League is to-day so firmly established. For many years he trained, with amazing success, the Hunslet Carr schoolboys, and there is no doubt that those boys developed not only a high degree of technical skill, but also many fine qualities of self-discipline, self-respect and self-control. We wish him every happiness in his retirement.

We also tender our sincere thanks to ... Mr R W. Blayney of Hull, who represented his District on the County Committee for a considerable time, and who, in his retirement, still continues to work so wholeheartedly for the schoolboy cause.

Yorkshire Schools' Rugby League Handbook, 1948-49

One person who shouldn't be forgotten is Norman Jolly who worked tirelessly for many years and was responsible for the school set up.

Norman was retired before I became involved but he was there in a President's role and his steady words of wisdom had a great influence on me. Norman was a Life Member of English schools.

Talking of characters - Warrington Schools had a great supporter in the famous rag and bone man - Ronnie Paget. Ronnie was an ever present at all the games both home and away and his volunteer role was very much appreciated when sometimes there were two other adults with the two teams.

One of my lasting memories of Schools RL is the friendships it developed with colleagues from other towns. My involvement as a town team coach, referee, NW Counties delegate and English Schools representative enabled me to meet regularly with a lot of great characters. Ray Unsworth, Dave Mallen and Denis McHugh from Wigan were all great friends and it was a pleasure to attend matches and meetings with them. St Helens had Jim Forshaw and Jim O'Reilly whilst Leigh had Zac Knowles and Bert Causey. Don Preston was at Salford and the unforgettable Fred Howarth was at Oldham. Perhaps the most interesting relationship for a lot of Lancashire teams was with Hull Schools, who at one stage were affiliated with Lancashire!

In 1982 I organised the first ever exchange for Warrington Schools with Villefranche de Rouergue. This was after I had hosted the French team, Pamiers at Culcheth. The exchange was brilliant in that it saw parents getting involved for fund raising and tour organisation and they then volunteered on a more permanent basis. We had some wonderful people involved at that time, Neville and Jean

A typical school's action shot as Jonathan Wright tries to break the cover.

Morrell, Peter and Sheila Connelly, Dave and Angela Horrigan to name but a few.

Mike Loftus - former grade 1 RFL referee - emigrated to Australia and heavily involved with schoolboy tours to G.B.

Schools rugby league was first played in Hull in 1901 and one of the first teams was from the Sutton School. Between the Wars, the Association grew in strength and there emerged strong teacher personalities and even stronger teams. Who will ever forget Courtney Street School? Under the influence of the legendary Stan Adams, they won the Yorkshire Shield for nine years, a record broken in recent times by Hunslet's Belle Isle. Perhaps the greatest of the

Barry Pugh, selected from Barrow and district, swaps school uniform for North West Counties U11s kit in 1994.

dedicated teachers was Alan Sproxton, whose interest in the game covered a period of some 50 years. Others of note were Bob Blaney, Charlie Simpson and Syd Coverdale and the schools of the time were Lime street, Crowle street, Lincoln Street, Blenkin Street, to name but a few.

In the thirty three years since those war years, two stalwarts stand out as the 'giants', the late Bill Ablett and our Life Member, Geoff Kirby. It was Bill, working closely with lan Sproxton, Stan Adams and George Atkinson who got the game going again in 1945/46. He devoted his whole life to the game, going on to become the chairman of English Schools' Rugby League in its early years of existence.

Geoff Kirby led the Association as its Secretary for twenty years, through what could be truthfully called the 'golden era' - the period of the Secondary Modern School. From the early 50s to the Comprehensive reorganisation, Geoff controlled this great expansion in the sport. No one could foresee the end of these halcyon days but the demise of the Secondary Modern School in 1969 almost killed off this Association.

Bill Watts

I was appointed Senior Master at St Paulinus in 1955. Initially, I was surprised by a lack of motivation from the senior boys to school life in general and sport in particular. There was an undoubted pool of talent requiring channelling and encouraging. It was a soccer playing school in which moderate success had been achieved but this sport did not fulfil the intense passion and desire to achieve which is inbred in so many families in the Heavy Woollen District. Introducing disciplined physical contact sports was the answer. Rugby league football and boxing was the catalyst and we went on to produce highly competent performers in both sports.

In 1958 all the local RC secondary schools were merged into a brand new school St John Fisher RC High in Dewsbury. The new head Mr Duffy wanted to put the school on the map straight away. Derek Brown suggested forming a RL team that would aim at winning the prestigious Yorkshire Schools U15 Cup. In 1959/60 they reached the semi final, but were well beaten on the big Headingley pitch by Kirkstall Road from Leeds. In 1960/61 Fishers reached their first YSRL final, played at Odsal as a curtain raiser to the RFL Championship in front of a crowd nearing 40,000 and beat Thornes House from Wakefield 14-5.

Deryck S. Brown

The sight of the late, great Bill Ablett leading the Hull Boys from the tunnel is a lasting memorial to a man who gave 42 years of his teaching life to the game he loved so much.

Wembley, 1976

The contents of the book, its production and the end result, a curtain-raiser before the Challenge Cup final are dedicated to Steve Box. Steve was Chairman of the Association from 1986-1990 and only stepped down from office this year due to the onset of a sudden illness. At the age of 36 he achieved so much in such a short time for our Association.

Steve was one of the first teachers in Calderdale to gain the Level One, Grade One National Coaching Award. From this he encouraged colleagues to take the award so that children within Calderdale would benefit. Steve was made a District Coach for the Halifax area on the National Coaching Awards Scheme, and helped organise many Level One courses. It was Steve who helped create a link with Halifax Rugby League Club and the Schoolboy Association, which has become vital to our development. It was with great pride that we heard that Fiona asked that donations be made to our Wembley Appeal instead of flowers for the Funeral.

Halifax Schools Wembley Brochure

Arthur Spencer, that most urbane of men had the distinction of being the only person to hold the office of chairman twice. He was a decent, fair minded, courteous man, always anxious to be fair and honest. He was a strong advocate for, and defender of, Schools' RL. He spent a life-time promoting Schools' RL in Barrow and it is a cruel irony that in the season he died, Barrow Schools' RL reached its very first ESRL final.

Gilbert Dautant, Vice President of ESRL and President of *Jeu a Treize* was a tireless worker for the game in France,

Andy Farrell, ESRL skipper, greets his French counterpart watched by Colin Murray (chairman, ESRL), Lord Derby and French Directuer de l'equipe de France Cadets, Gilbert Dautant.

Gilbert's contribution to the Cadets cannot be over-estimated. Problems could always be solved when Gilbert was around.

Ray Unsworth

It was with wry amusement that many schoolteachers read Brian Batty's article in the Wigan programme of Sunday, 13th March. Brian, it seems, had received a dig in the ribs for not handing out a fair share of the credit to clubs producing our stars of the future. He proceeded to put the record straight by naming players 'produced' by one of our local BARLA clubs. These players spent up to two years being groomed in the stables of the local BARLA organisation! Of course, the fact that they spent six years before that being groomed in the Wigan Schools' RL escaped his notice. However, teachers have learned to live with this reportage. For years dedicated coaches have given up time and effort providing games of rugby league for thousands of boys (not just for the skilful few), instilling in them a love of the game so that the majority would either continue playing or enjoy watching in a more knowledgeable way.

Dennis McHugh

Very few schoolboys would recognise the name W. H. Hirst, let alone would have met the man. George was not a teacher. He was nevertheless a great believer in our aims and a dedicated worker for our cause. George had been a regular attender at meetings from 1948.

He was elected a Life Member in 1957 and in 1963 became the first non-teacher Chairman of the Leeds Schools' Rugby League. George, particularly in his later years, derived almost as much pleasure from his involvement with the schoolboy code as he had done in his many years connected with the professional game. The Hirst residence was a haven for rugby league enthusiasts - a welcoming handshake from George, tea and cakes courtesy of Stella, you never failed to be inspired by the ideas, enthusiasm and optimism; you always came away revitalised.

The name Hirst will never be lost to Leeds Schools' Rugby League: the under 11 League Championship Trophy and the under 11 City Player of the Year Trophy bear the inscriptions 'W H Hirst Trophy' and 'Hirst Award' respectively.

W. H. Hirst 1912-1990

In 1932, the new Manchester Road Boys' School opened and Bert moved there to teach mathematics and PE. He formed a rugby team immediately and it is no doubt, due to his efforts that Manchester Road became the centre of schoolboy rugby league in Leigh. He saw his first county match in 1934. In 1937 his school team reached the final of the *Daily Dispatch* competition.

The match was played at the Leigh RFC ground at Mather Lane but Manchester Road were beaten by Parr Central of St Helens. I spent a very enjoyable hour with Bert at his home when he opened his 'case' containing programmes, handbooks, photographs, and he talked about boys that played for the county teams that he coached. He said, "Best pair of half backs were Alex Murphy and Jackie Edwards in the county match of 1954. Best Lancashire side played at Craven Park, Hull, in 1951. We defeated Yorkshire 43-5, Peter Marner, later Lancashire CC captained."

Tribute to Bert Causey

Castleford captain, Alan Hardisty and team-mate Keith Hepworth began their wonderful partnership at the age of ten. Failing the 11-plus, the pair went to the Ashton Road Secondary School, and into the hands of physical education teacher Mr Percy White.

White, nicknamed 'Chalky', winced when he first set eyes of 'Hardisty's lot', for physically they were rather small. 'They weren't much to look at - there were no big or strong ones - but they were a pleasant, cheerful and likeable lot who developed fine spirit and great skill at games.' White started at Ashton Road in 1946, after leaving the Army. He knew nothing about rugby but he got down to the task of learning.

Of Hardisty, White says: 'In his first year he already had that uncanny ability to read tactical situations, size-up openings, beat men, and use the ball with hand or foot. Heppy was different - a slow starter, but he was well worth

NORTH WEST COUNTIES SCHOOLS' RUGBY LEAGUE

(President: J K Hampson, Esq., M.A.)

75th Anniversary Dinner

(Lancashire Schools' Rugby League: 1913–1976.
North–West Counties Schools' Rugby League: 1976–1988)

Friday 22nd April 1988,
at Haigh Hall, Haigh, Wigan.

RECEPTION 7.30pm. DINNER 8.00pm.

Poached halibut and entrecote steak on the menu and Colin Welland as guest of honour waiting for'. In 1955 the Ashton Road team brought the Yorkshire Schools Cup to Castleford for the first time.

Percy 'Chalky' White, revered teacher

I went along as an interested observer to the 1974 High School All England Sevens and they won it. When we got back, the Headmaster, Mr Hughes, arranged for the cook in the lower school to do us a celebratory dinner in the evening with some invited guests. My contribution was to write a poem about it which Mr Hughes suggested we get a copy for all members of the team.

Peter Hirst

The kids work their socks off. They live and breathe rugby. But, also, it's helped with their behaviour. We'll use the rugby as a sanction. It's quite hard sometimes because I'm trying to pick my best side. It's turned a lot of lads round. Rough diamonds, brilliant lads, who go on to great careers. Rugby has channelled a lot of them. So much is relationship with the kids. My day, as soon as I walk in, even if I've got something to do, I'll have kids following me telling me about the games. They live and breathe it.

Lee Hudson

(First ever touring schools) Cup Final weekend is looking quite interesting as Reg Pearce's Walton-on-Thames U11s face York Schools U11s on the Saturday morning. Reg, the Ealing coach, has put a lot of hard work into introducing the game in the West London region and beyond. Having started off Ambleside and Forge Lane schools in Walton, he's now working on two other schools in the area, as well as helping teachers to coach R.L.

Down South Newsletter – Spring 1979

Primary school rugby owed a great deal to Mr David Price, Head of Beaumont Junior School for reviving the game in the 1970s.

G.E.Bannon

In 1994, I resigned and Don Preston took over, until his untimely death which meant that I was, once again, asked to coach the national team, an appointment I accepted, but would rather not have had the opportunity. Don will be sorely missed, not only for his massive contribution to the life of Salford Schools' RL, his wise counsel as an officer of the ESRL, but also for involvement at international level. A fitting tribute to the man is the fact that Swinton Parish Church could not hold the vast numbers who turned up to pay their last respects.

Dennis McHugh

7

*

Stars in the Making

The St Helens Touring Team at home against the Salford Boys gave a sparkling exhibition. They had two discoveries, including one boy who is perhaps the best and biggest forward St Helens schoolboys have produced, Huyton.

Daily Dispatch, 18th May, 1935

That day was absolutely fantastic. I remember getting on the coach and doing the famous coach-ride into Wembley stadium, with all the fans walking around. I was sat in the dressing rooms tying the laces of my boots and I remember thinking that I wasn't very nervous at all, it was just another game. But once I got out onto the Wembley pitch in front of all the fans then it hit me how big the game and the event was. It was a really special day and something that will never leave me.

Sophie Cox- the first girl to play at Wembley and subsequent Olympian

We weren't very successful because we didn't have any facilities for training. We had just a tarmac playground and if we wanted to play on a field we had to walk to Glasshoughton down to the cricket field. I remember plain as day when we played against Wheldon Lane and this little lad kept getting

Winifred Holtby School, Hull, unbeaten between 1991-6. This year 7 side included Richard Horne (middle row, second right).

the ball and running rings round us. And, after he'd done it so many times, the teacher said, 'Right, no try!' 'Why not?' he said. 'I'm disallowing it cos you must learn to pass the ball, otherwise you're never gonna be any good. And this was Roger Millward. It's the teamwork aspect of it. You've all got your own skills. It teaches you that you can't do things on your own if you want to be successful.

John Harvey

The value of schoolboy rugby league has proved itself to the Southern Amateur Rugby League, which this season has recruited several fifth and sixth formers from the Peckham Manor and Daneford schools into the Nag's Head and McEntee open-age sides. Impressive performances have been made by Leroy Underhill and Victor Welch (Peckham Manor) and Valentine Butt, Lee Toman, Colin Pitcher, Shafkot Ahmed and Barry Geary (Daneford).

Another milestone was achieved in September when Brian Howarth's Brunswick Boys Club side from Fulham became the first youth club from London to go on tour. They played a couple of matches in Yorkshire against a York school and then the Hunslet Boys Club U13s as a curtain raiser to the Hunslet v Wigan game at Elland Road.

Down South issue 4 - autumn 1979

In 1986 Stephen Mullaney thrilled the television public by scoring a long-distance, solo try as Wakefield Schools defeated St Helens 17-0 in the U11 curtain-raiser at Wembley. Tragically, Stephen died in a road traffic accident the following year and, as a tribute to him, the Year Seven game was given the name of the 'Stephen Mullaney Memorial Game.'

Champion Schools Brochure

In 1981, we were aware that Bonfire Night and Town Team training were going to be on the same night. Would we still be expected to train? Someone plucked up the courage and asked the coach. We should have known the answer, 'If you want to play on Saturday, you train on Thursday'. As Bonfires were lit and fireworks set off, we were on the old Robin Park playing fields going through yet another set of unopposed rugby practising set pieces; rehearsing new moves; no one was going to risk losing his place and facing a serious fight to get it back. To miss Bonfire Night was a sacrifice but the rewards were tenfold. I can still smell the wintergreen, still hear the sound of studded boots on concrete floors, and still feel the pre-match butterflies in my stomach. I wouldn't swap it for anything in the world. We may only have been schoolboys but we got the chance to play in the footsteps of rugby legends.

'Playing in the Footsteps of Legends' - Marcus Sumner

In 1992 I played at Wembley in the curtain raiser. We watched the Challenge Cup final from close up and from that day on I wanted to be a rugby league professional.

Kevin Sinfield, most successful Leeds Rhinos captain ever and led England in 2013 World Cup

Winning is very important to both players and coaches. That is why points are awarded for scoring tries and goals. However, long after the result of the match has been forgotten, the friends gained on and off the field will be the longer remembered. And the enjoyment from playing, watching, or officiating will last forever. I look forward to the same pleasure that I have had ever since, as a seven year old, I was introduced to an oval ball at school.

Ray French

On John Holmes: The trouble was, with him being so proficient, the rest of the kids would give the ball to John if they could. So instead of him doing one thirteenth of the work he would do about half. He was very modest, didn't say much. I met John at a function years later. He remembered me and came and had a little chat. I was really chuffed.

Ken Breach, teacher at Burley National

When John left school at fifteen, all the lads who played with him subscribed and bought him a cup as a memento. The Holmes family had a chip shop on the ring road. Years later, after John had won every honour the game had to offer,

The 1993 French Cadets including Catalan Dragons coach Laurent Frayssinous (third row, third on right).

---

some of the Kirkstall Road pupils would go to work in the shop to earn a few extra bob. One day, one of the lads told how John's father had taken him into the front room to view John's trophies. He told the pupil that the cup John was most proud of was the cup that was presented by the lads at the school all those years before.

Dick Pickard

Keith Bell was little, stocky - weighed a ton and half on your shoulders - but by God, he was a good hooker. I'd been picked as captain of the Castleford and Wakefield Town Team against Leeds and Hunslet and it was a curtain raiser for the Yorkshire Cup Final - Hull and Featherstone. The Hull team had Johnny Whiteley in it. I didn't think a year later my first team debut would be against Johnny.

Doug Walton

Schoolboy rugby league - Heavy Woollen style

Much public attention has been focussed in recent months on the high standard of play which has been shown in the televised Sunday games by players of U17 and U19 years of age. If the records of the star players in these games are examined, one finds that invariably they learnt their rugby league football at school. The schoolmasters are to be complimented on the successful way in which they have instilled the fundamental skills of the game into their charges and I am sure they themselves are deriving pleasure from the youths' subsequent successes. The amateur movement in rugby league is almost completely dependent on them.

Letter to 'Rugby Leaguer 'newspaper

In one tour alone - that 1958 Australian trip of which I was a member - there were twenty players out of that party of twenty-six who had graduated from schools rugby league.

Vince Karalius in his book 'Lucky 13'

Rugby league in schools is so important. You build friendships, improve your communication skills and most importantly develop discipline. Travelling to new towns and schools is an invaluable experience, and away matches tend to provide the best memories from my school days. You played sport and had fun with your friends.

Phil Clarke, current Sky Sports analyst

My earliest memory of Schools' rugby league was one of fear, going for a trial for the Wigan U11s Town side. To go down to Robin Park on a Saturday morning was the dream of every rugby fan. The atmosphere, quality of rugby and the rivalry between the towns was fantastic.

Andy Farrell, Wigan superstar

John Bartlett keeps a video recording of an old game. It is of an U14 team he once coached at Our Lady of Mount Carmel School in Salford. Tall and skinny, Adrian Morley looked almost ungainly. Morley makes a tackle, smashes a finger, picks himself off the ground and instinctively goes to the mark to do his defensive duty. Once the opposition move the ball away, Morley looks at his shattered finger, signals to the referee and leaves the field. Within minutes he is on his way to hospital. He came from neighbourhoods where discipline wasn't high on the agenda but couldn't wait to develop self-discipline. 'John had so much enthusiasm for the game that you really wanted to be in his team. We loved rugby league because of the way he coached it,' Morley said.

David Walsh - 'Sunday Times' article 28th March, 1999

I cannot remember at which point during the 1975 season we as a squad were informed of our selection/invitation to play against Widnes Schools' town team in the first ever curtain raiser to the Challenge Cup final at Wembley, but all conversations with those associated with the game, with family, friends and teachers seemed to be punctuated with 'you don't know how lucky you are' and 'you will remember the day (10th of May 1975) for the rest of your life'. A few of the events as I recall them are: sharing a coach down to London with our opponents, a depressed young Mike Gregory who would not play in the big game due to an illness, walk around on the pitch and another 'telling off' for trying to remove a piece of turf the size of a large dinner plate as a souvenir, meeting with, and the autograph of Ken Dodd, who would lead the traditional communal singing, an overnight pre game stay in a hotel with an ice making machine - providing both frozen missiles and excellent way to have fun, mischief and to calm any pre game nerves; a distraction that was taken from us with stern words to the effect of 'Do you realise you are representing Wigan?' Arriving at Wembley really early to get changed in the room with the marching band, a game we lost 8-0 due to two tries from Raymond Galloway and David Hume - both names forever engraved in my mind.

Joe Lydon, Widnes, Wigan and Great Britain flyer

I was fortunate to referee the English Schools Cup final in 1983 and Bobby Goulding had then signed for Wigan. I penalised him for feeding the scrum and his immediate comment was, 'feeding, feeding! Do you know who I am?' I called his bluff, 'No' I replied, 'but my name is Hawley, this is a whistle and that's a penalty!'

Frank Hawley

My teacher colleagues and I never set out to 'make'

Sheffield trio proudly display their medals.

professionals. Laurie Brookfield, a Courntey Street boy, is the first name I link with schoolboy rugby and the professional clubs. He played for Hull boys as hooker and Hull K.R. for many years. Trials for Yorkshire Schoolboys were held at York one year and a rather impudent youngster refused to let the predominantly West Riding element overawe him. He even volunteered to take the goal-kicking. He was Peter Flanagan.

Geoff Kirby, secretary of the Hull Schools R L Association

I was selected to represent Wakefield Schools on the trip to France. I was 14 years old at the time and one of the youngest in the party and it was also my first time abroad. I couldn't get home quick enough to tell my parents the news. That moment was like playing at Wembley and being picked for Great Britain all at once. I was playing loose forward at the time for school and city teams, but being younger and smaller than the other forwards in the party, I didn't think I would make the Test team in that position. On arrival in France I told the coaches that I was a hooker, and I made the side for the game in Perpignan, that was the start of my rugby career as a hooker.

David Ward, the first 'Man of Steel'

Widnes Schoolboys v Barrow Schoolboys. A representative eleven selected by the Widnes Schools's League, journeyed to Barrow on Saturday, to meet the Barrow Schoolboys' team. Widnes kicked off against a strong wind. Barrow pressed strongly, Fallowfield scoring at the corner. Barrow continued the pressure, long kicks spoiling their efforts. Later Hocknell scored. Hosker saved grandly time after time. Lipear played brilliantly, but the backs could not make headway. From a mark in front of goal an unsuccessful attempt to add points was made. With the aid of the wind, it was expected that the Widnes team would make havoc of the home team, but this was not so.

Inter-School League report - 7th April, 1909

St Augustines Catholic High School, Redditch crowned Year 11 Midlands Champions, 2009.

Oakwood Junior school in 1962/3 had an exceptional team, we went through the full season undefeated. As champions of Warrington we went on to represent the town in the Lancashire cup and managed to win it. I have an official photo of the team with all the cups on. I can still name every player. I also have some action shots my father took of us playing Long Lane. I have a newspaper cutting and photo of both teams from the Ashton Cup final. I also still have the winners medal from that game.

Gordon Sloane

I went to Rivington Road School which had always been a hotbed of rugby league. John Mangle was our teacher and one of my main memories was beating Parr Central in the Ellison Cup final. I was captain of the St Helens Schools' teams at both Senior and Intermediate levels. I remember two lads in particular from that town side; Mike Ahearne who took part in the 'Gladiators' series on ITV, and Mike Cowley, who went on to play professionally with Oldham and Swinton. I was selected for Lancashire Schoolboys and played centre, marking Ellery Hanley at Barrow. From the match I was selected for England Schools, at full back. My dad had watched every game I played at schools' level, home and away, and I remember him being over the moon when the letter came informing me of my selection. The match was played at Whitehaven. I had never played full back before and I was a little nervous. The French put up a 'bomb' after about two minutes and I took it. I was quite confident after that. Henderson Gill scored two tries, and his dad came in after and showed his delight by singing calypso songs!

Neil Holding, St Helens entertainer

Burton Borough, Telford the Midlands' top side at Year 7.

I started in 1949 at Evylyn St School (Primary), 11+ year. Our form master was Mr Norman Jolly who was 'Mr Schoolboy RL' in Warrington and Lancashire. One day whilst taking PE he said to the boys, I want 13 volunteers to play against St Mary's. You, you, you, etc and Brindle you can be captain. I can remember when we played on Victoria Park after school we would run from Beamount down Battersby Lane with our school bags full of books and our playing gear.

Alastair Brindle, Warrington star

My first school was Temple Street. They started a team, we were playing against older boys. We learnt a lot from getting beaten. The teacher, Mr Robson, was a fanatic. We used to play in Wigan's strip - red and white - and it was strange, but it made you feel more special. At Cas High School, Mr Hirst did a pen picture for an Open Day. It was motivation for me

- 'good rugby player, wish he'd practise more with a ball and less with a bag of fish and chips.' They talk about it should be the taking part not the winning but every kid plays to win. You can't say: 'We'll have a match and we won't count the score', because even if you don't they will. There was no dirty play, it was played in its purest fashion. It was still tough but there wasn't room for it in schoolboy rugby. What you got was the mentality of winning, the basics of teamwork and that it takes all sorts to make a team.

Barry Johnson, ball handling Castleford prop

Vivid in my memory is that wonderful display of tackling by little Peter Riley, the Leigh full-back, when he brought down the big powerful Oldham forwards in the 1934 Lancashire Cup final at Watersheddings. That was the only occasion on which I have seen a visiting player of the losing side cheered and carried off the field shoulder-high at the end of a match. Gerry Helme was the Leigh schoolboy captain in 1936, but he was only selected as reserve for the county match on the Belle Vue Rangers ground, Manchester. Another great scrum half who also only acted as a reserve for his county schoolboy team was Billy Horne of Barrow.

Cyril Smith, Chairman NW Counties RL

I wasn't regarded as anything special and didn't seem to get noticed until I was about 14. I say this to encourage those lads who sometimes just 'make up the team' - keep trying and your time will come! I know it was so unexpected when I started to get picked for teams. I suddenly started to improve. Then in 1992, I got the call up for England Schools. I couldn't believe it, but was I proud! For most of us it was the first contact with the demon drink and the French national game of trying to get the English drunk!

Iestyn Harris, Welsh great of the modern era as player and coach

John Joyner was so big, we picked two sides and me being about as big, it meant that I had to try and tackle him out of the game without thwarting his interest. Occasionally I let him slip through and score a try. I was 25 and he's 13! That was the only way we could make some kind of a contest. I started teaching rugby, for which I'd got no credentials. I'd played soccer at school and rugby union and Melvin Mason had every trick in the book. At 12 he had it all, he even taught me the rules. I wasn't a coach, all I was, was a kind of mentor. I trained them in the sense that I got them fit. They simply needed somebody to take them and show interest. If you went two or three weeks without being able to get a fixture for lads who were absolutely dying for them, then you felt like a fraud. What amazes me is that talking to people like John, they hark back to a schoolboy match. 'Do you remember when so and so scored that try in corner?' And I'd forgotten. They've played hundreds of professional matches - far more memorable I would have thought than a school one, and they could remember some nuance.

Roy Homer

The Town Team had some great times. We beat Hull in the 1996 English Trophy final. I was lucky enough to be picked for North-West Region and then for English Schools. I was overjoyed - it was such an honour for my school and family. The following year I was made captain of the national team, the ultimate accolade, and it was in this environment that I really started learning. I suppose that was the spark that ignited my career. English Schools gave me a profile and I'll always be grateful to them for everything they did for me. My England coach, Don Preston, was a massive influence on me rugby-wise and in life generally. An ex-pro, he knew a lot about the game and talked sense. I listened. Don got us focussed and prepared and then just told us to go out and

Feltham Community Sports College reach the national semi-finals in 2006.

---

enjoy it. It seems like a cliche, but that's exactly what we did. Don respected his boys. I remember that in France the lads who didn't get picked for the Test sneaked out to drown their sorrows. I still chuckle at the thought of Don going off in his suit to carry home some unfortunates and coming in with his best trousers ripped.

Kevin Sinfield

The England squad had been together for the first ever training session run by ESRL at Warrington before setting off for a snowy Lake District venue at Whitehaven. Two changes were enforced on the original selection – T. Grundy (Wigan) being injured and E. Hanley (Leeds) falling ill on the day. France too had to make changes, their biggest loss being loose forward and captain Guasch.

ESRL v France, 1977

Full page *'Independent'* article in the Education supplement entitled, 'Tackling the North-South divide' with a focus on Brentwood County High School, Essex.

Gary (Hetherington) offered me the job doing schools coaching. I absolutely loved it. It was me and Daryl Powell. It was great to be able to tell all these kids about rugby league. We went to some great schools, we went to some tough schools. I always remember going to Hinde House where there was this kid called Naseem Hamed who was prancing around the field saying he was going to be the next champion of the world and bigger than Mohammed Ali. I said, 'I don't care about what you're going to do - today we're playing rugby so get yourself round this field.' The kids had seen us in the press and would be excited by meeting us. When they went home they'd still be talking about it. I still get it when I go out round town - people say 'you came and coached me at school' and I say 'when was that' and they say

'20 years ago!' All the cheeky kids I used to sort out with the tackle shields. We used to say to the teachers 'put an 'X' on the heads of any kid you want sorting out'

Mark Aston, Sheffield Eagles factotum and Ireland coach in 2013 World Cup

At school, you didn't just play rugby or soccer, you played handball, basketball, netball, badminton, we could do anything with a ball 'cos that's how we were brought up. If somebody threw one to you, you just stuck your hand out and caught it. Every kid at Ashton Road School could all pass, catch, kick and tackle and do all kicks - the grubber, the place, the drop kick. Percy had a game played to toughen you up a little bit called 'murder'. You played in the gym on a wooden floor and he had a mat at each end of the building and what you had to do was get to the other team's end and get the ball on the mat any way you could. You could foul or jump on the opposition whether you'd got the ball or not. It made you look after yourself because if you didn't, you didn't survive. Percy was at all the games. He was there on a Saturday morning in his own time although we struggled when he was referee because he was such a fair man he'd let no-one say: 'They won cos Percy White's reffing.' If it came to a big decision, he'd give it against us.

Alan Hardisty, Castleford's favourite son

Wigan School's U16s travelled down to play London Schools in the first round of the prestigious English Schools Rugby League Trophy competition. Boasting four county players in their side, including Lydon, they are one of the three top town teams in the country and on the morning of Saturday, 3rd Nov at Morden Park, Surrey were in no mood to make compromises. The experience of Chris Swann, brother of Leigh professional Malcolm, Kevin Egan,

Castleford High Girls celebrate a Year 8 success.

grandson of the mighty Wigan front row man Joe and Ian Gormley, grandson of miners' leader Joe, coupled with the all-round talents of centre David Wood, who finished the morning with four tries and seven goals, put Wigan in front by 31-0 at the interval. London's tackling had been good, hard and occasionally spectacular. One interested spectator at the game was John Stopford, the former Great Britain winger, who now coaches one of the Wigan schools sides.

'Wigan Schoolboys Have No Peer' – Eifion Collins, 1979

8
*
Pushing the Boundaries

In 1969, a French Schools' side from Marseilles visited Wigan under the leadership of Monsieur Marcorelles. To honour their visit a dinner was held in The Grand Hotel at which The Mayor and Mayoress of Wigan were present. The Mayor that year was a lady. Monsieur Marcorelles addressed the gathering in French (he could not speak a word of English) and made presentations to the dignitaries. The Mayor was quite taken aback to receive a bottle of after shave. Continuing with his speech, Monsieur Marcorelles had the French boys standing up cheering and laughing. Our interpreter looked somewhat abashed and said that what he'd said was, 'Go back to where you are staying, get a good night's sleep, but don't wait up for me. I shall be visiting the brothels of Wigan.'

Ray Unsworth

The fortnight beginning with the Cup Final weekend was a particularly interesting and varied one for the boys of Daneford School, Bethnal Green. Not only did a large group of them go to Wembley in the afternoon but also, in the morning, entertained Holy Family High School, from Thornton, North Liverpool, on Hackney Marches.

Down South newsletter

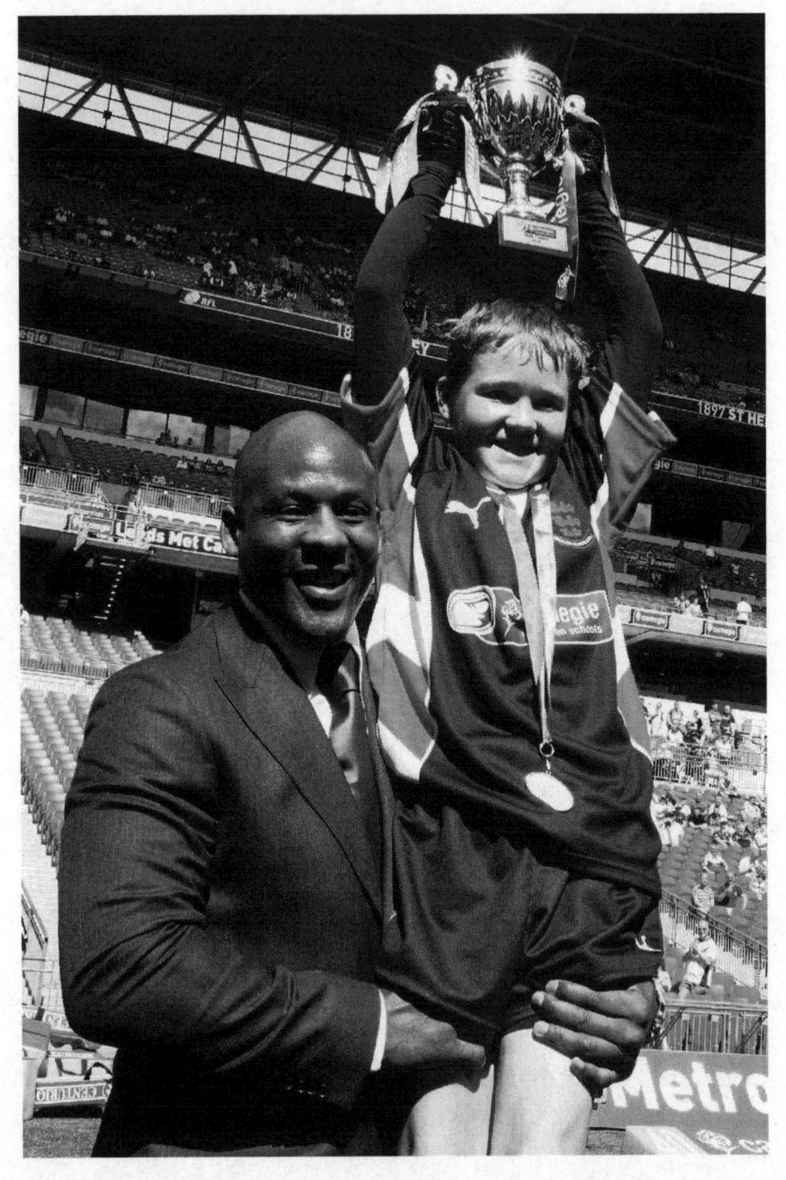

The perfect memory, Dowdales Year 7 captain, scrum half Joe Satterthwaite, is hoisted aloft by trophy presenter and league superstar, Ellery Hanley after victory at Wembley.

1947-8 saw York's entry into the county association. The first match against Dewsbury and Batley was lost 14-5, but as a result of his efforts Alan Magson of Manor was selected to play for Yorkshire against Lancashire at St Helens in April, 1948. Tang Hall were the first school to represent York in the County Cup competition, but they were defeated by Kirkstall Road School. 1950-51 York really 'burst' on to the county scene, the Sproxton Trophy was won outright and York again had three boys in the county side. Ken Bowman, for Fishergate was particularly pleasing as Bowman organised the Fishergate School team on his own as there was no teacher available. From 1959 onwards a new school began to emerge as a power in York, Beckfield.

York and the County Year Book

Rugby league often appeals to many schools purely on its merit of accessibility. The sport is welcoming to not only those who have a historical involvement in the game, but the new, emerging and intermittent schools who are afforded access to rugby league as and when their curriculum allows. We hope to follow in the footsteps of the likes of Feltham and Brentwood who have only a handful of years experience between them, but due to the transparent and principled nature of the sport, are encouraged to partake in local, regional and national competitions.

James Giblin, School Sport Coordinator at Twickenham Academy

Rugby league began in Castleford Area Schools in 1934. Until that time football was the schools game. Prominent in the beginning were Walter Smith a Castleford R.L. Club director, W.B. Davies and Jim Parkin. A meeting was held at St Joseph's RC School which was attended by John Wilson the then Secretary of the Rugby League. A promise was made that participating schools would have jerseys

On the burst at sun drenched Wembley, the culmination of Year 7 Champion Schools competition.

supplied by the Rugby League. There was no official league organised at first. Also during the years up to the war an Evening Schools League was formed based on players turned out from local schools. In 1964 the schools involved were Junior (11 yrs) and Senior (14 yrs). Senior children left at the end of the term in which they reached leaving age. A

team established before Xmas could be decimated for the New Year matches. Smaller championships could not be run. Eventually these lists included fixtures for an U13 age group which became known as Intermediate.

Percy White

Schools rugby league offers something for everyone.

The Leeds and Swinton schoolboys' own 'Wembley' at Wandsworth yesterday morning resulted in a good win for Swinton by 9 points to 6. Isherwood of St Mary's School, was the Swinton star. Two of his three tries were scored after running from near his own line. The tries for Leeds were scored by Buckle (Quarry Mount School) and Rooks (Hunslet National)

'Swinton Schoolboys Win ' – May 1932

One Welsh school, Brynteg, won the Year 7 Champion Schools final back in 2005 at the Millennium Stadium. Many of their players are now professionals with two of them, Rhys and Ben Evans signing professional forms for Warrington and were in the full Wales squad. When Brynteg won, they were one of just a handful of schools from Wales who entered. Now we have schools from Pembrokeshire across to Monmouthshire. We also have girls competitions which again is showing how much progress we're making.

Mark Jones, Wales RL

You can pretty much guarantee that a school based in an area of high social and economic deprivation such as Brixton will receive a similar if not the same experience as a school at the higher end of the social scale who are located in the likes of Richmond. We continue to break down barriers for our sport.

Ebony Blake, RFL development officer

Starting in 1977-78 a schools RL competition existed in Hamilton, Scotland. Henry Callaghan had been asked to organise team sport for a group of schools and because of his own background he chose rugby league. The new intake from the Primary Schools was very promising and playing at a much higher standard than at a comparable stage last season. Stars of the show up to now are undoubtedly the U11s. They have played four, won four, scored 80 points and have not had a single point scored against them, a remarkable achievement when one considers that the opposition has all come from established rugby league areas. We had so many boys down from local secondary schools asking us to form an U14s. On December 11th they played their first game against Egremont Rangers and although they were beaten 21-0, they gave an excellent account of themselves. The Primary Schools Championship competition for the George Fairbairn Trophy is now in full swing. Five teams are involved and they will play against each other throughout the season on a league basis. The five are: Chatelherault, Low Waters, Hamilton Saints - combination of St Johns and St Marys, Blantyre - combinations of St Blanes St Ninians and St Josephs and

Different Class

Greendyke Giants – Edinburgh. Entirely as a result of the efforts of Anne Orr, Honeywells have very kindly donated a magnificent silver Cup and fifteen medals. Any Scottish primary school will be able to enter a team for the competition which will initially take the form of a tournament, all the rounds of which will take place on the same day. Since the beginning of the season Steve Strang has been doing sterling work in spreading the game in Edinburgh. He has now formed a club based on one primary school - Greendyke Giants. There is tremendous enthusiasm among the boys who are always immaculately turned out in a splendid all-white strip with green and yellow Vs and green numbers.

'Who can stop Hamilton Lions?' article

Have you heard the one about the Englishman, the Irishman and the Scotsman who took a party of schoolboys to play rugby league in France? The Englishman is Ron Morgan, the tour manager, the Scotsman is Jack Lee, the business manager, and the Irishman is Bernard O'Hara, who is the team manager for the second time. School teacher, Mr O'Hara has the most unlikely background for a rugby league official. The head of geography at All Saints' Comprehensive School, played hurling and Gaelic football in Ireland and came to Huddersfield from Cork in 1957 only because he could not get a job in his native country. He soon became addicted to the thirteen-a-side code. The party flies to Bordeaux and will be based at a youth hostel in Lezignan. The Sports Council have given a grant to cover expenses for the international game, but the rest of the cost is borne by each association, who have raised £50 for each representative.

Huddersfield Examiner

Building on the success of recent years the Carnegie Champion Schools competition in the South of England has once again seen some significant developments. The boys' game has grown by over 30 per cent, London and the South has now engaged over 1,000 schoolboy teams in the initiative. The most notable annual developments have been recognised in Hertfordshire with the introduction of the St Albans and Hemel Hempstead sub regional competitions. The Essex competition has also witnessed an increase in uptake by 400 per cent.

Andy Gilvary in 2011

In 2005 Outwood Grange College began a ten-week exchange with Rockhampton High - Brisbane when former England Schoolboy Taron Wildley and James Davey began the annual exchange. The success of this venture has snowballed and seven students per year are now jetting off

Joy in South London as Ravenswood School pick up their first national trophy.

Luke Metcalfe, scorer of the first try at the new Wembley stadium, dreams of one day lifting the Challenge Cup there

to Australia as soon as they finish their year 11 exams. Due to the high numbers, Mackay High School - near Brisbane - have become involved in hosting. Two students per year return the favour and are hosted by Outwood families. In 2007 and 2009 Mackay High school toured England with an U16 team playing Outwood Grange and Castleford High before venturing to Lancashire and playing a Harlequins development team.

Outwood Grange brochure

In 1979-80, Brunswick Boys, Scott Lidgett U15s recorded the first ever victory by a SSYCARLA team over a northern side, beating tourists Delph Hill (Bradford) 26-14. Ambleside Avenue in particular continued to flourish under Reg Pearce, staging a 'Day of Rugby' and a tour of Hull. In 1980-81 Daneford played Langdon Park in the curtain-raiser to the inaugural Oxford v Cambridge Varsity Match at Craven Cottage. In 1982-83 a London U18s team lost 0-22 to French Schools at Maidstone and also toured France (accompanied by an U15s team), winning most of the games. In 1977-78 a schoolteachers' side known as Stockwell Manor played a few friendlies and a teacher-&-student team from Sibford near Banbury played one match at Oxford.

Mark Newbrook

At Parkside on Saturday, by permission of the Hunslet Rugby Football Club, before a crowd of about 3,000 spectators, the newly-formed Dewsbury Central School team was beaten by a Hunslet team by eight points to five. Donald Ward (who is a son of Ernest Ward, the trainer for the Dewsbury Schoolboys) 'sold the dummy' brilliantly and cut through, after which he transferred to Fitton who ran half the length of the field and scored a brilliant try.

Dewsbury schools debut- report

It is perhaps indicative of England v France Schoolboy rugby league games that the first French visit to England was arranged on a traffic island in the middle of Manchester's Piccadilly, when two non-French speaking Englishmen met a Frenchman who spoke no English! Many of the professional game's leading players got their first taste of international competition in an English Schools shirt, but for others the Schools international will be the high point of their sporting life.

The first English Schools tour to France took place in the autumn of 1967. There was no precedent for selecting such a team, so each association affiliated to the English Schools RL was asked to nominate one player to make the trip. The very first England - France Schoolboy international was played in Perpignan, on November 5th 1967. England won 17-2. It was five years before further contact was made, when, in the Spring of 1972, a party of 17 French boys and four officials arrived in England. The 'Test' match was played in Hull, and England, again, proved to be too strong. The following season, schools exchanges between England and France were complicated by the arrival of the never-to-be-forgotten Australian schoolboys. For a while afterwards, it seemed possible a reciprocal visit down-under was on the cards, but financial considerations made this impossible. In March 1974, another invitation to tour France was accepted. This was described as the first 'really organised tour.' England beat France in the 'Test' at Villeneuve-sur-Lot by a convincing 36-10 margin. Reports of that game mentioned the fact that the English manager had to take his boys off the field to cool down for a while after Kevin Dick had scattered the opposing pack. In 1975, stung by their reverses, the French put together their strongest side to tour. A squad of 32 boys included Bourret, at 16 years of age, who was already an occasional team player for XIII Catalan, and the young prodigy was the outstanding player of the Test, played at Warrington, which France won 14-9. The French went through that tour unbeaten. The French boys (known as the Cadets) returned to England in 1977, and were billeted at Liverpool University. Hunslet schools became the first individual schools to beat a touring team - 16-9 at McLaren Field, Bramley.

Ron Morgan, ESRL official

The season 1978-9 saw Ambleside School's first organised fixtures. An Inter-House competition was held - 120 boys taking part at U11s, U12s and U13s. This represents about

Girls in action, an area of significant schools rugby league growth over the past ten years.

half the number of boys here. A most successful innovation. Rugby league was introduced to the locality by means of an exhibition morning. Seventeen teams took part from seven schools and a youth club.

Eifion Collins

A perfect illustration of battling against the odds by future Castleford hooker Daryl Clark, an epithet for the schools game.

There is no doubt that rugby league is played in many more schools than it was - during curriculum time as well as in competitions. However, the profile of Schools' Rugby League has changed. There are many more sports on offer and, whilst school R.L teams may play in high-profile competitions, most will play far fewer fixtures than they did in the past. When I started teaching in the late 1970s, schools had regular fixtures, played mostly on a Saturday morning, or mid-week at the beginning and end of the season. Teams would play around 20 fixtures. Nowadays most school teams do not reach double figures unless they are amongst the most successful sides in regional and national competitions. 2000 saw the last full season of representative Schools' rugby league, where schoolboys could represent their town or city and their county at U11, U13 and U16. This system provided logical stepping stones to enable players to be challenged at their own ability level, and also led to much missed rivalries - both local and cross-Pennine. The system made way for the Service Area. The Champion Schools tournament is one of the biggest success stories in British rugby league. When it was re-launched in 2002, with the Rugby Football League in partnership with English Schools' Rugby League, 304 teams took part.

Stephen Boothroyd

Away from a few enthusiastic teachers and club volunteers organising training and friendly matches against local schools, rugby league in schools only grew initially around the efforts of the professional club London Broncos and the RFL; with the sport expanding rapidly around the turn of the millennium. In 1994 Broncos brought Australian school teacher Tony Rea over on a playing contract and in conjunction with the RFL appointed him as a Rugby League Development Officer taking the sport to schools around the West London area, as the youngsters were hooked on the big tackles, runs with the balls and diving in for tries. The RFL appointed John Kain and Caro Wild as Regional Manager and Oxford Rugby League Development Officer respectively in the late 1990s which furthered the blue print in the sport in Southern England. I joined Phil Jones and Graeme Thompson at the London Broncos, who now played in Charlton, South East London, in progressing the sport in schools. Tony Clubb and Louie McCarthy-Scarsbrook were found through the schools coaching programme in the area. With the RFL, London

Skolars and London Broncos all having full time staff, a coordinated approach could be taken and secondary school cups for the whole of the London and the South put into place. This coupled with Champion Schools meant unprecedented growth in the schools sector. Red Hall produced nice glossy brochures advertising the game and competition. We picked up countless schools from simply writing to every single one and asking them to reply if they were interested in playing. This was the first time this had been done and the response was amazing; we quickly moved to over 100 school rugby league teams regularly playing. There was a great spirit of togetherness at the time.

Chris Thair

Dewsbury had offered to host the visitors for part of the stay in their Dales holiday centre but that must have seemed in the wilderness to our visitors who were eventually put up elsewhere. The game against Yorkshire was lost 22-2 but visiting officials were upset by our interpretation of the rules and Mr Howarth had to use his persuasive powers to settle the problem amicably off the field. For the Test at Hull, All went well after the game but much later a late night phone call brought Messrs Teale and Lee to Hull to the local police station to help restore amicable relations between the irate proprietor of a Chinese restaurant and some misunderstood French officials!

French arrive - 1972

What they needed was someone to go in and communicate with schools and set the programme going. It was very successful. At one time I think we had about 100-odd schools where there were various tournaments. To be honest, the PE teachers welcomed us with open arms. Sheffield Eagles being sponsored by Whitbread for three of four years was a real bonus, because when we had the teachers meetings at Penistone Road there were free cans of beer. That really set the programme off! The Sheffield Schools U11s playing at Wembley in 1993 was a great achievement. It really lifted the profile of rugby league in Sheffield. One of my earliest memories was taking a Sheffield Schools team to play at a nine or ten-a-side Yorkshire Schools competition. Most of the kids were from Tapton - a nice school. Nice kids, but they got a hiding. The kids needed the experience, we needed to get a schools rep team going at some point, but there was such a gap between the kids who were playing the game regularly up in West Yorkshire and these kids in Sheffield who've run about with a ball for an hour.

At that time, English Schools RL was only concerned with the curtain raiser at Wembley and the international game in France and the hospitality that went with it. The development of schools and individual school kids was just not on their compass. They couldn't comprehend that. In many ways we were the outsiders coming in and there was a bit of resentment at that. I tried to get Sheffield Schools at Wembley from the start. It took five or six years to win them round to the idea, and even then it was touch and go.

There certainly wasn't any template and there weren't any resources. In fact, I distinctly remember going to the Rugby Football League when I started and telling them I wanted a load of posters to put in schools featuring a picture of Ellery Hanley or whoever. They gave me the number of Andrew Varley, the photographer, who wanted to charge me £100 a picture.

One of the best things I did down there was run a coaching course with the PGCE students at Sheffield University. There were only about 15 or 16 of them, but the spin-off of that was fantastic. I know one or two of them got jobs in Peterborough and Norfolk or wherever and they were teaching rugby league to kids in their schools. They're intelligent people, and you can sell rugby league to them quite easily.

Tim Butcher - Sheffield Development Officer, 1987-93

In 2002 St John Fisher embarked on a tour to America, New Zealand and Australia which included netball and soccer as well as rugby league.

The tour was known as the Anza Tour. Forty four students and seven adults made the trip which lasted for almost four weeks. The idea came after we won the ESRL U12 competition in 1999. We thought that this particular group of kids were a bit special and we wanted to take them a stage further. Walter and Gail Paul, the parents of Henry and Robbie co-ordinated the New Zealand leg of the tour. The children were billeted out to different families including former Bradford centre Shontayne Hape.

The three rugby games in Australia were against Trinity Bay High School, Aspley Rugby Club and Westfields Sports High School. We played out of our skins but Westfields were awesome in terms of skills, speed and awareness.

Bernie Preece

We have received great support from both well-known personalities and from grass-roots aficionados of the game, the 'Down South' newsletter, on subscription at £1 per annum, being instrumental in making our existence known in R.L. circles throughout the world.

Visiting teams from Newlands Y.C. (Hull), St Helens YMCA, Huyton Tigers, Holy Trinity H.S. (Thornton, N. Liverpool) and York Schools have all provided experienced opposition for our boys who have responded with a marked improvement in their own game. Daneford School's tour to Scotland brought much praise and the Brunswick Boys Club

Alan Hardisty, one of the best to grace the sport, returns to his old school at Ashton Road – now named Smawthorne Henry Moore Primary – at the launch this project.

(Fulham) U13s are all set for a pre-season visit to Yorkshire to play a York School and a Hunslet Boys Club side. The pioneering spirit was certainly in evidence when Stockwell Manor School took part in a R.L. competition along with schools from Staffordshire and the North at Butlins Holiday Camp, Minehead, Somerset.

Dave Part

They're trying to make rugby league branch out from the M62 and they've done an incredible job, because we're now travelling in the National Champion Schools down to London. We played Holyfield, Feltham. We've had some good games. They're getting stronger and stronger.

The Welsh sides are particularly strong. They're not like us with three schools within a few miles. These schools are very, very big on their own. They have a large base of pupils

Some of finest exponents of schools' rugby league either as players, administrators or teachers join with the next generation to mark the start of the archive-gathering

to pull on. We went down the night before, stayed in Monmouthshire and the team had a brilliant time.

Lee Hudson

Talented youngsters Joe Capless, Jake Connelly, Scott Fleming and Jack Young will be heading down under to further their rugby league education as part of the ongoing partnership between Castleford Academy and Mackey State High School, Queensland. The partnership has flourished over the past four years and after the current exchange a total of 17 students from Castleford Academy will have taken on the once in a lifetime opportunity. The players will fly out to Australia at the end of June after their final GCSE exams and will be staying with Australian families for the duration of the trip. Head of PE Lee Holmes said: "Although it will cost around £2,000 per student to participate in the exchange, it is a fantastic opportunity for these young lads. We have already had some donations and sold numerous raffle tickets."

Pontefract & Castleford Express, June 2013

9

*

History Makers

The secretary (W.O. Smart) reported that twenty four schools had joined the Union, including sixteen of last year's members. An emergency sub committee was appointed consisting of the Officers and six gentlemen. It was resolved to produce a printed circular containing an appeal to the public for subscriptions towards a fund for providing trophies and medals. Resolved that the city be divided into three districts North, South and East and that the championship of the city be decided by the top school of each district playing on a neutral ground.

Leeds Schools Rugby Football Union Minute Book - First AGM - General Committee Meeting held at Green Dragon Hotel, September 3rd, 1903.

There is a gaiety in Paris in the springtime that makes the heart beat faster and our schoolboys here in St Helens are all agog with excitement at the thought of the thrill that will be theirs with its amusements, shops, boulevards and gardens. To gain contact with French schoolboys in sport will not only promote friendly relationships, but will also mark the beginning of annual visits. The Rugby League have arranged all the matches and the grounds and have been responsible for the publicity and advertising in France. This will be a pioneer tour, and we in St Helens are very delighted at the opportunity given to us to lay the foundations of rugby league in the French schools. We are confident that with our experience and enthusiasm we can be of definite help to the French schools to organise their rugby competitions on the right lines. The secret of successful rugby teams is love for the game, good organisation, and sound coaching.

The thirty-six boys are drawn from 18 different schools, and there will be five masters to look after their welfare. Mr 'Cuddy' Pennington, one of the oldest 'evergreen' sportsmen of the town, will travel with the party as trainer. The Rugby League Council have appointed their efficient courier, Monsieur Charles Bernat, to travel with us as guide and helper throughout the tour. The St Helens Boys, when playing against the French Boys' team, will wear the jerseys (Saints' colours) kindly presented to them by Mr Fred Jones, ex-chairman of St Helens.

'St Helens Schools Tour de France Pioneers set out tomorrow',
by W.N. Ashburner, 1935

Over 150 budding Rugby League players descended upon London Broncos' Roehampton training ground for a community tournament run by Broncos Foundation Team. School teams made up of year 8 students from Richmond, Hounslow, Kingston and North Surrey battled it out on an afternoon which showcased the talent that is emerging in the country's capital. In the Hounslow Grand Final, Rivers Academy faced Feltham Community College. Pre tournament favourites Grey Court came up against Twickenham Academy in the Richmond Grand Final. Southborough High School and Hinchley Wood successfully negotiated their way to the final of the Kingston and North Surrey group. The winners from each of the borough's pools went on to face each other for the right to represent London

Presenter of the medals in 2010, Terry O'Connor, is entertained by the Year 9 player of the match after Brooksbank from Elland defeat St Benedicts of Whitehaven at the Hillingdon Sports and Leisure Complex

in the nationwide leg of the Carnegie Champions Schools out of which Surrey's Howard of Effingham Year 7s became the first school side to play at Wembley in the Challenge Cup curtain raiser.

'Budding London Broncos' – report by Hashim Piperdy

1946-47 - The Lancashire v Yorkshire County game is played at Swansea. A trophy donated by The *Daily Dispatch* was presented to the Lancashire Captain after a 12-6 win.
1954-55 - Lancashire games against Cumberland and then Yorkshire played at Leigh under floodlights for the first time.

Notable Lancashire dates

They were on average nine months older than their English counterparts and they were a formidable machine. Their training regime shocked some, amazed others and made many realise that their approach to the game was professional in almost every way. The physio at Oldham RLFC where the Aussies did a lot of their training commented that they used so much ice due to the ferocity of their training that they would have been better off at the North Pole.

ESRL Secretary, Ron Morgan wrote 'This party of fit 17-year-olds showed a dedication to, and an awareness of rugby league seldom seen before at any level in this country. Selected after extensive trials, the boys prepared for the trip by two weeks' training that would make a commando shudder. In the three match Test series, they scored 103 points for with only 5 against, making the final points tally; 402 for, (made up of 108 tries and 39 goals), with just 17 against. They only conceded one try in the very last match played in London. Schools' rugby league it may have been, but rugby league in its entirety in this country received the biggest ever wake up call. The warning signs had been there.

'The day the Aussies came to town' -
Australia Combined High Schools tour 1973

The inaugural winners of the Salter Shield were Pemberton Colliery School in 1909. The individual prizes for winning were substantial. The photograph of the team shows silver watches and chains and gold centred silver medals.

Coalopolis to Pie Eaters

Panic was a recurring theme from the beginning to the end of the first Schoolboy tour of France. My first panic attack came when I caught a stray boot or elbow in a tackle causing a cut eyebrow, so had to come off during the final trial at Warrington, thus jeopardising my selection. The second when the family overslept causing me to miss the train to London. My dad drove at break-neck speed to get to Crewe, the next rendezvous point. The third when, having been billeted out for our evening meals with French families around Carcassonne, and being looked after by a French rabbit farmer and his wife, I spoke very little French, and they spoke even less English.

We travelled to the ground and saw posters which told us that we would be playing against 'Cadets'. The rumour spread quickly that we would be playing against boys two years older and the French side seemed to be all moustaches and big hairy legs. Panic attack number four; we were relaxing after the Test match when the coach, Eppie Gibson informed me that as captain, I had to reply on behalf of English Schools' Rugby League at the formal celebration dinner. He also mentioned that it would be a good idea if I could speak in French. A kind lady rescued me from attack number five by translating my speech as I went along. The last panic came when I presented my Mum with her present of two prized white long-haired pelts from the French rabbit farmer. Her face was a picture when she opened the box and a mass of maggots tumbled out onto the best carpet.

'The beginning of l'entente cordiale in schools' - Graham Mayor

Ten Barrow schoolboys have been chosen to act as official ball boys for the Rugby League Challenge Cup final at Wembley. Walney School sportsmaster Dave Milburn broke the news to the lucky lads this week. 'The news came out of the blue. To say I am delighted is an understatement. I am very thrilled for the boys.' The ten lads and two teachers will travel down on the Friday and will be handed track suits and trainers from the Rugby League. They will stay two nights at the Ladbrooks Hotel on Empire Way. However, only one night's accommodation is provided.

Paddy McAteer – 'Off to the Ball' newspaper article

In 1926, when the rugby football shield was won, the team scored 306 points during the season, not a single try being scored against the school. That year four of the team played for Lancashire against Yorkshire, Barnett, the school captain being the Lancashire captain.

Beaumont School Yearbook

I played for Long Lane juniors in 1971/2. We lost one game all season winning the league, Miller 7s and the Ashton trophy. Our 7-a-side team was the Warrington team for the North West 7s. Our rugby teacher was Harry Pace and woe betide any player caught with a football the week before a rugby match. We were on a 10p each bonus for winning the Ashton trophy against St Augustines at Wilderspool.

Eddie Woodall

On Easter Saturday, 3rd April 1999 Wigan's famous Central Park stadium staged its final international. It was an U16 match between Great Britain and France. Several members of the British team have gone on to star in Super League.

Line-up: Richard Mathers (Leeds), Chris Hill (St Helens), Chev Walker (Leeds), Gareth Morton (Widnes), Alex Wilkinson (Oldham), Danny McGuire (Leeds), Billy Joe Edwards (Wigan), Jamie Bovill (Hull), Andy Crabtree (Wigan), Ben Thornton (Leeds), Jason Netherton (Hull), Adam Sullivan (Hull), Sean O' Loughlin (Wigan); Subs: Shaun Briscoe (Wigan), Damian Simms (Wigan), Malcolm Riley (Wigan), Aaron Smith (Leeds), Rob Burrow (Featherstone).

The British won 52-8. Skipper Crabtree ended the afternoon with a personal tally of 20 points. The two French tries were scored by Christophe Moly and Yannick Brousse.

'British Schoolboys win at Central Park' report

Swinton won the Lancashire Schoolboy's Cup at Station Road. Great credit, however, must be accorded the Leigh boys. They fought courageously and with more than a little skill. Weight told against them. This was reflected in the amount of possession secured from the scrums. The second row forwards stood out by reason of physique and merit. Among the three-quarter line Kenny, the Swinton captain, appeared to tower over colleagues and opponents. The

Swinton centre was Stanley Evans, son of Jack Evans, the former Swinton and England player. What a record it will be if this lad eventually wears the club colours carried with such distinction by his father and grandfather.

The winners each received a wristlet watch, and the losers a wallet. Mr Anderton said Jubilee Year would be a memorable one for schoolboy football. Inter-county matches between Lancashire, Yorkshire and Cumberland had been instituted. He looked forward in future years to a 'curtain raiser' at Wembley and the time might soon come when there would be international matches between England and France.

'Leigh Display Fine Pluck' – report 2ndMay, 1935

I played on the inaugural tour to France in 1967/68. I scored four tries including a hat-trick in half a game when I came on as substitute in St Gaudens. We stayed in a youth hostel in the old city of Carcassonne, when we weren't playing or preparing for a match we had to go and live with a local French family, mine owned a garage in Carcassonne.

Bill Strickland

Two Dewsbury and Batley Schools R.L. players who have this week experienced the thrill of recognition for the first time by the County selectors are James Colleran, of Woodsome Estate, Batley, and Raymond Patrick Heaps, of Hume Street, Batley, members of Batley St Mary's School U15 team, this season's schools league champions. Their selection is an honour for the school for, as far as records reveal, these two boys, both aged 14, are the first representatives of Batley schools to play in the County schoolboys team, although it is claimed that Frank Gallagher, former famous international, previously earned this honour.

'County Schoolboy Honours' report -1951

Disappointment is a woefully inadequate word to describe the expression that was written all over the face of Barrow Schools' coach Dave Wright when the final whistle blew at Wilderspool stadium. Wright, who has devoted a large part of his life to the Barrow Schools over the last three years, could only stare at the dust by his feet. A few yards away on the pitch the Wakefield coach was celebrating with his lads who had just been presented with the cup. If the PA had played Yvonne Fair's 'It Shoulda Been Me' the picture would have been complete. 'It just wasn't to be,' whispered the local photographer who plodded from my side to arrange the after-match team picture. 'I don't know whether I'll be able to summon a smile,' murmured Barrow schools' secretary Alan Craven, although he buried his own emotions and cheered his players up. Poor Dave Wright said hardly a word. On the car park, the sun sparkled form all the Barrow registration plates and caught a reflection in the Shaw Hadwin coaches. Up in the grandstand mums, dads and friends gazed down at the scene with thoughts of what might have been. The young men who were still draped in the Barrow colours they had worn with great pride, collected their runners-up mementoes with dignity, a couple even managed a wave to the supporters above. Wakefield had some big hard lads, but the Barrow tackling was breathtaking. No game this, for faint hearts, either on or off the field. Bang! Down went the bull-necked Yorkshire number eight Booth. Smack! Down went the long-striding second row Lockwood. Wright and Craven, immaculate in their sweaters and ties, were out of their seats on the touchline shouting advice. The players glanced back beneath sweating brows and nodded to each fresh instruction. The girls in the crowd issued an extra special shriek whenever Paul Gardner got the ball. When he actually scored in the 30th minute there was near apoplexy. Wright was disconsolate after the whistle. 'I'm still a bit disappointed, but I don't think we let anybody down. But me and the lads have come a long way together in three years'. Among the spectators was Barrow Braves coach Dennis Ramsdale. 'They showed a great deal of character and commitment. The support was tremendous - I just wish they would get themselves down to Barrow more often and shout like that.'

'English Schools Rugby League Cup Final - Barrow 24 Wakefield 28' report by Frank Cassidy

1981 was the year the French schoolboys U16 side gained only their second victory on English soil when defeating their English counterparts 12-8 at Naughton Park, Widnes. Defeat was a shock to the English, even greater when you consider their line up in which every member of the squad signed professional. Statistics prove that around 80% of the English schools side will sign professionally at the age of 17 and by the time the boys are 18, this figure has risen to around 90%.

'The Talent Production Line' - David Ord

Outwood Grange Year 7 defeated Castleford High 20-12. Jacob Ware became the first player to score a hat-trick at the new Wembley.

Champion Schools, 2009

Hull's rugby league schoolboys retained the Yorkshire Schools Shield, which they have held for twenty years at the expense of Huddersfield Schoolboys at the Boulevard. The Lord Mayor of Hull (Alderman Watson Boyes) kicked off in a match which resulted in a hollow win for Hull by 44 points to nil. The locals revealed wonderful schooling in the finer arts of the game.

'Huddersfield Schoolboys Overwhelmed' – report 12th Feb, 1927

The result of the Schools curtain-raiser never seems all that relevant - but for the record Rochdale took the 1983 Steve Mullaney Memorial Trophy, beating Sheffield 12-6. More important, it was another successful PR exercise.

A timely reminder for the people of Sheffield that kids in the city now play rugby league as well as football. There was no doubt who stole the show, with the PA announcer informing the crowd at regular intervals that the first girl to play League at Wembley was No. 1 for Rochdale. With a special feature in the programme and *Grandstand*'s coverage featuring on her, everyone's eyes were on Sophie Cox. She had a good game, setting up the match-winning try for hooker Craig Smith with an intelligent and accurate long pass.

'Sophie starts match winning move' by Andy Wilson, Guardian

History was made in this district when the first match in the much criticised U11 League was played at Cross Bank between St Mary's and Eastboro' Junior School. Since the Committee decided to run this league, many people, including well known local authorities on the game, condemned it as being too much for lads of such tender age. These lads gave an exhibition of courage and resolute tackling that would have shamed many a professional team; and six were eight years of age. They enjoyed every minute, and as one spectator said, 'There can't be much wrong with the R.L. game when lads of this age put up such a performance.' A new venture has been launched and it remains now to spread it to those schools who declare the game is too rough for their pupils.

D.S. Brown, Treasurer, Schools R.L. (December 1950)

Much has been made by the use of the sin-bin. English Schools' introduced this at its inception, 15 or so years before the Rugby Football League.

ESRL Brochure

Scott Lidgett U15s from Bermondsey made Southern Schools rugby league history by becoming the first ever Southern side to overcome northern opposition. Their opponents, Delph Hill (Bradford) had opened their weekend tour with an impressive 23-6 win against Dick Sheppard School from Tulse Hill. However, the tables were turned the following day when Scott Lidgett coasted home to a well-deserved 26-14 victory through the strong running of Khan, Bines, Facer and Slack, Parsons being successful with four conversion attempts. Ambleside Avenue (Walton-on-Thames) played gallantly on Saturday as hosts to the more experienced Newland YC from Hull. Ambleside were in action again on Sunday afternoon taking on the Daneford (Bethnal Green) U15s side on Hackney Marshes in the final of the Daneford PTA Challenge Cup competition. Size and age difference told in the end as Daneford registered a 42-3 victory. Next weekend 140 London schoolboys will be going to Wembley to watch the Rugby League Challenge Cup final. Thornhill High School from Dewsbury have arranged to play London U15s on Hackney Marshes and Holy Family High School from Thornton, North Liverpool will be taking on Ambleside Avenue and Peckham Manor at U13s level.

Daneford School - Press Release – April 1980

Mel Ward, coach of the successful Year 7 girls side St Thomas More, has been delighted with her side and by the competition as a whole. 'The girls had a fantastic time at the festival and are really looking forward to the challenge ahead at Cardiff. Currently we are training twice a week. We can't get enough rugby league at the moment and the girls will be going to watch the Skolars play and hopefully gain a few tips.'

'This is the first time a girls' competition has taken place.' says David Raybould, RFL Women and Girls Development

England coach Steve McNamara hands out the man of the match prize after the annual Year 7 final at Wembley

---

Officer. 'The Girls Powergen Champion Schools has been a massive plus and it will become a driving force behind much of our development work during the next five years.'

Powergen Champion Schools Brochure

The '*Open Rugby*' Cup, our premier competition, attracted 41 entries, and was climaxed by a magnificent final at Headingley between St John Rigby College (Wigan) and Castleford High School. It was played in an excellent spirit and was splendidly refereed by John Holdsworth. It was a particular feature of the game how frequently the wingers on both sides were brought into play. St John Rigby came within a whisker leading 8-5 with two minutes to go. But Castleford's unconverted equalising try by centre Green led to a four try onslaught from Castleford in extra time.

The disappointment was that only a small number of

teams completed their minimum requirement of 10 merit league fixtures, too many teams did not arrange sufficient fixtures for the first two months of the season and found themselves struggling to reach the target in the winter months. Despite this St John Fisher HS (Dewsbury) were worthy premiership winners and it was good to see Barnsley Sixth Form College contesting the final against them.

The first BUSCARLA sevens were held at Station Road, Swinton and the competition was won by St John Rigby College. The event was sponsored by the Midland Bank, who have kindly agreed to renew their sponsorship. Central Park was the venue of the first inter-county match - both teams produced a high standard, a tribute to the coaching of John Ireland and Martin Crick respectively.

May I pay tribute to all those who have contributed to the success of BUSCARLA - especially Peter Deakin, whose efforts as Development Officer have been outstanding.

Stephen Alderson -

Report of BUSCARLA's activities for the first full season.

On a freezing Watersheddings night, December 6th 1972, we caught our first glimpse of the Green and Gold jerseys of the touring Australian Schoolboys. A real feeling of expectancy hung in the cold mists. We were not to be disappointed. The speed of the attack and vigorous defence spelled total commitment. One boy in particular tested the patience of the referee on several occasions with his physical approach and became the first player to spend time in the 'sin bin' which English Schools introduced years before the RFL. His name? Les Boyd! The first ever Ashes Schools' Test was played at Central Park, before a crowd approaching 3,000 - marvellous considering the time of year and the counter attractions of soccer at Springfield Park and live RL on TV.

Ray Unsworth

The coach was Paul Metcalfe (Westmoor Middle) with Pat Ganley assistant. Additional coaching was provided by the then Leeds skipper and Great Britain star David Ward and Ernest Wilby, a well known figure in local amateur circles in the heavy woollen area. A strong Widnes side won 15-1 with Bobbie Goulding and Terry O'Connor amongst the points scorers. The Dewsbury point came from a Paul Hinchliffe drop goal - the first kicked in a curtain-raiser. Overthorpe teacher Diane Stewart made history by becoming the first woman to join the parade on the Wembley turf.

Wembley, 1983

92 per cent of the England U18 team which whitewashed the Australian Schoolboys at the end of 2002 for the first time, played at first team level.

RFL Statistic

The 1969/70 Cas lads inspired a generation. They even came back with the cup to our school! You got that image: 'I want that.' Then Tony Marchant and I were taking the cup back to school in front of an assembly and it's a fantastic feeling. I wanted it to be exactly the same.

Barry Johnson

Their predecessors made history exactly 100 years ago. And today, the current young rugby stars of South Crosland CE Junior School will get their taste of the spotlight. The youngsters will do a lap of honour at the John Smith's Stadium in front of an expected 10,000 crowd and millions of TV viewers. Their parade during the Huddersfield Giants v Leeds Rhinos Challenge Cup tie comes a century after the school team clinched the Northern Union Rugby Cup. Their victory came on May 3, 1913, when they defeated a team from Hull's Lincoln Road School 8-6 at Belle Vue. And they did so in thrilling fashion, coming from 6-5 down to win with a last-minute try. Details of the victory – and of the semi-final triumph against Kirkstall Road School from Leeds – emerged during a research project into rugby history. Brian Heywood, of the Huddersfield Rugby League Heritage Project, said: "It has been fascinating to uncover some of the history of the sport. The South Crosland school team of 1913 were all conquering. In March that year they won the Hoyle Cup, against teams from all over Huddersfield, and went on to compete in the regional finals which saw them triumph. The final was actually played as a curtain raiser to the Rugby League Championship final – the equivalent of today's Grand Final – and fittingly it was won by Huddersfield.

"We have been back to South Crosland School to re-enact some of the drama of the final and the kids had a great time. Schools' rugby league is still very big in Yorkshire but a century ago it was huge. There must have been about 100 teams playing in the Huddersfield area, but obviously when war broke out a year later a lot of them were decimated."

The school logbook dated May 3, 1913, read: "Today the boys' Football Team played in the Final for the 'Yorkshire Schools' Cup'. Their opponents were Lincoln Street School, Hull and after a hard struggle, our team emerged victorious. The winning try was scored in the last minute by Donald Jessop – a really magnificent effort. It is the first time the latter trophy has been won by any school in the Huddersfield & District".

Article in Huddersfield Examiner, May 2013

*

Afterword by Gary Hetherington

I was introduced to rugby league by my uncle, Tom, who took me as a nine-year old to Castleford home matches as a reward for doing his garden on Saturday mornings.

And there, at Wheldon Road, I developed an immediate and deep fascination of and affection for everything about the game – the grounds, players, history and most of all my beloved 'classy Cas', as they were to become known.

The game dominated my childhood and certainly my time at school. I persuaded Mr Taylor, the Head Master of Hightown Junior to let me organise teams to play in PE lessons, and playtimes became mini rallies and goal-kicking competitions. At that time, the prospects for lads in Castleford who weren't academic was a life underground at one of eight collieries in the town, but for me there was never any thought other than a job in rugby league and so I knew I'd better get good at something and the sport offered me a lifeline.

In my last term at Junior school, like everyone in my year, I failed the 11-Plus exam and thereby missed out on going to Grammar School. My parents were disappointed and I pretended to be but I was so excited at the prospect of Whitwood Mere Secondary Modern because they played league and had turned out lads who'd made it in the pro game – like Ian Stenton and Wilf Newton. On arriving there, I was fortunate to come across Roy Bell, the Geography teacher and keen coach, and a young Roy Homer, who taught History and had also grown fond of the game. They coached the rugby teams and were to play an important part in my development. We played in PE lessons and I remember receiving individual coaching, particularly from Mr Bell who taught us the basics of the game and especially how to tackle. His favourite player was Clive Dickinson, the Cas hooker who was a fearless tackler.

Roy Homer, noting my enthusiasm but chubby physique, also introduced me to weight lifting after school which helped improve my shape!

In those days, school numbers weren't large and each year had probably 15 or so boys who enjoyed and excelled at sport. The rugby team tended to be the same one as the soccer and the cricket sides and we would all compete at the various athletic events in summer. It was a terrific environment.

Mel Mason, who starred for Featherstone Rovers and then Leeds in the 1975 Premiership final and Geoff Wright were a bit older than me and the stars of the senior team. We had John Joyner, Roy Bratt and Bob Gaitley but Whitwood Mere were probably the weakest of all the 10 local schools who played against each other on Saturday mornings. Lads at others seemed much bigger than us, and we couldn't understand why they had hair in places we didn't!

Castleford Boys Modern were particularly fearsome, with 14 year old giants like John Vodden, Harry Boyer, Billy Wild and tricky half backs in Steve Ferres and Gary Smith. North and South Feathertone included ruffians like Mick Gibbons and Keith Bell.

Normanton boasted Neil Goodwin and Ross Bailey while Ashton Road; who had previously produced Alan

Hardisty, Keith Hepworth and Malcolm Reilly, had Peter Downham, Des Kerry and Steve Pincher in their ranks and Pontefract Carleton had a terrific stand off in Ken Johnson.

It was a highly competitive league and this was, of course, replicated in almost every other town in the county.

The highlight was selection for the Castleford & District team, who came together to play against other town teams in the knockout competition.

The school teachers who ran their own sides used to come together to select the squad and they would all travel with the team. The likes of Percy White, Jack Smith, Don Whittaker, Roy Close, John O'Neil and Jack Appleyard were legendary characters who did so much to fashion the lives of hundreds of youngsters. Their enthusiasm, dedication and caring for the boys was inspirational.

Travelling to play against Hull, Leigh, Hunslet and Leeds on a Saturday morning were great adventures for me and I can still recall the thrill of being involved. Of course, playing for the school and the town team also brought its own status and I remember a real sense of pride when the Head Master, Mr Crossley announced in the school assembly that our school had been represented by four boys in a recent victory over Hull schools.

I have a lot to be thankful to schoolboy rugby league for, in particular, those teachers who coached, organised and inspired the boys. It provided me with so many unique experiences and also a confidence that I could do well at something and sport gave me an interest, a passion and a good deal of discipline too. Its value was to have a lasting impression on me and when my wife Kath and I formed Sheffield in 1984, we realised that for the game to prosper in the City, it had to have roots in schools.

In the early days of the Eagles, myself, Daryl Powell, Mark Aston and some of our overseas players attended local schools and introduced what was then an alien game to them. It was a novelty for the establishments concerned but we found an enthusiasm among pupils and some teachers who picked up the mantle and slowly introduced rugby league to the curriculum. It was a particularly proud moment for us when the Sheffield Schools appeared at Wembley in the Challenge Cup final curtain raiser in 1993.

On coming to Leeds three years later, I was excited to be in and part of a rugby league city with such heritage, the Leeds & Hunslet Schools Rugby League Association was legendary. Leeds Rhinos are active supporters and the work of the Leeds Rugby Foundation in schools has made a difference.

It is so refreshing to see new schools take up the game with both girls and boys enjoying the challenge and we are very proud that there is more rugby league played through schools in the area now than at any other time since the 1950s. My hope is that current players get as much enjoyment and satisfaction from the game as I have.

GARY HETHERINGTON
JANUARY 2014

*

The Graduates

It's a thankless and futile task imagining what 'the best' schoolboy selections might be – indeed, many players will have peaked while at school and not been noticed thereafter.

But, looking back through the ESRL handbooks at those who have graduated to the highest ranks of the sport, these nominal, subjective ensembles at least give a flavour of the talent that has been nurtured through the schoolboy ranks.

A fictional Schoolboy touring squad has been selected by some of those who have worked with these elite performers at that level after such trips came into being in 1967, the baseline date for this exercise.

They are split into Test and midweek teams purely so as to be able to include more of them and some are in unfamiliar positions, but the ones where they first came to be noticed in.

Behind these names overleaf is a long list of school coaches and administrators who are widely recognised by those included as having played a huge part in their development both as players and men.

TEST SQUAD

Shaun Edwards	ST JOHN FISHER	WIGAN
Henderson Gill	DEIGHTON	HUDDERSFIELD
Garry Schofield	PARKSIDE	HUNSLET
Ellery Hanley	CORPUS CHRISTIE	LEEDS
Leon Pryce	QUEENSBURY	BRADFORD
Andy Farrell	HAWKSLEY HALL	WIGAN
Andy Gregory	DEANERY	WIGAN
Sam Burgess	HECKMONDWIKE G	KIRKLEES
Kevin Sinfield	SADDLEWORTH HIGH	OLDHAM
Andy Platt	DE LA SALLE	LEIGH
Paul Sculthorpe	COUNTHILL	OLDHAM
Lee Crooks	SIDNEY SMITH	HULL
Phil Clarke	ST JOSEPH'S	WIGAN
Keiron Cunningham	BROADWAY HIGH	ST HELENS
Des Foy	ST ALBANS	OLDHAM
Danny McGuire	AGNES STEWART HIGH	LEEDS
Denis Betts	CLARINGTON HIGH	SALFORD

MIDWEEK TEAM

Rob Burrow	AIREDALE	CASTLEFORD
Mike Smith	GREATFIELD	HULL
Iestyn Harris	NORTH CHADDERTON	OLDHAM
Mike Gregory	ST JOHN FISHER	WIGAN
Bobby Goulding	FISHER MORE	WIDNES
Sean Long	DEANERY	WIGAN
Deryck Fox	THORNHILL	DEWSBURY
Shaun Wane	ST THOMAS MORE	WIGAN
David Ward	ST THOMAS A BECKETT	WAKEFIELD
Jamie Jones Buchanan	PRIESTHORPE	LEEDS
Lee Jackson	BRANSHOLME HIGH	HULL
Jon Wilkin	SOUTH HOLDERNESS	HULL
Sean O'Loughlin	ST JOHN FISHER	WIGAN

Mike O`Neill	BANKFIELD SECONDARY	WIDNES
Jonny Lomax	ST CUTHBERT'S	ST HELENS
Steve McNamara	SOUTH HOLDERNESS	HULL
Gareth Hock	ST THOMAS MORE	WIGAN

Coaches

Eppie Gibson	WHITEHAVEN
Walter Norris	WARRINGTON
Don Preston	SALFORD

Administrators - perhaps a difficult job keeping this squad in line

Barney O`Hara	HUDDERSFIELD
Bill Watts	HULL
Peter Dawson	HUNSLET/MORLEY
Tony Profit	WAKEFIELD
Roy Knowles	LEIGH
Ray Unsworth	WIGAN

Among those who have played in the Schoolboy's Wembley curtain-raiser, the Stephen Mullaney Memorial match and now determining the Year 7 Champion School are - Joe Lydon, David Hulme, Mike Ford, David Plange, Denis Betts, Bobbie Goulding, Terry O'Connor, Phil Clarke, Chev Walker, Kevin Sinfield and Sam Tomkins.

Stay up to date with all our latest releases at
www.scratchingshedpublishing.co.uk